RISC-V Assembly Language Programming
Learning By Example

By Yury Magda

To my wife, Julia

About the Author

Yury Magda is an embedded engineer experienced in designing hardware and software for Intel x86, ARM and RISC-V embedded systems. He is also the author of the books on designing embedded systems based upon various development platforms.

Contents

Introduction

This book is designed to be your comprehensive guide to learning RISC-V assembly programming by example. Whether you are a novice programmer stepping into the world of assembly language for the first time or an experienced developer looking to expand your skills into the RISC-V architecture, this book provides a thorough, hands-on approach to mastering this versatile instruction set.

RISC-V (Reduced Instruction Set Computer - V) is an open-source instruction set architecture (ISA) that has been gaining significant traction in both academic and industrial circles. Its simplicity, modularity, and extensibility make it an ideal platform for education, research, and a wide range of applications. Unlike proprietary ISAs, RISC-V is free and open, allowing anyone to study, modify, and implement it, fostering innovation and collaboration across the global computing community.

In all examples from this book, we use RV32 that is a 32-bit subset of the RISC-V architecture, designed for applications that require 32-bit addressing and operations.

Why Assembly Language?

Assembly language provides a clear view of what is happening at the hardware level, giving you ultimate control over your program's execution. By learning assembly, you gain insight into how high-level languages are translated into machine code, enabling you to write more efficient and optimized code. Additionally, understanding assembly language is essential for tasks such as debugging, performance tuning, and developing system-level software.

Programming is best learned by doing, and this book is designed with that philosophy in mind. Each chapter contains numerous code examples with detailed explanations accompany each example to ensure you understand the underlying concepts and techniques.

This book assumes a basic understanding of computer programming and familiarity with fundamental concepts such as variables, loops, and functions. Prior experience with a high-level programming language like C or Python will be beneficial but is not strictly necessary.

Disclaimer

While the author has used good faith efforts to ensure that the information and instructions contained in this book are accurate, the author disclaims all responsibility for errors or omissions, including without limitation responsibility for damages resulting from the use of or reliance on this work. Use of the information and instructions contained in this work is at your own risk. If any code samples or other technology this book contains or describes is subject to open source licenses or the intellectual property rights of others, it is your responsibility to ensure that your use thereof complies with such licenses and/or rights. All example applications from this book were developed and tested without damaging hardware. The author will not accept any responsibility for damages of any kind due to actions taken by you after reading this book.

Basic concepts

RV32 is a specific implementation of the RISC-V architecture that supports 32-bit addressing. Here's a breakdown of the key differences and specifics:

- **Bit Width**: RV32 specifies a 32-bit architecture, meaning it uses 32-bit wide registers, and addresses are 32 bits wide.
- **Register Set**: RV32 has 32 general-purpose registers (x0 to x31), each 32 bits wide.
- **Addressing**: Supports 32-bit memory addresses, allowing it to address up to 4 GB of memory.
- **Extensions**: RV32 can be extended with various standard extensions like M (integer multiplication and division), A (atomic operations), F (single-precision floating-point), D (double-precision floating-point), and others.
- **Word Size**: RV32 uses a 32-bit word size, while RISC-V as a whole can include RV64 (64-bit) and RV128 (128-bit) implementations.
- **Address Space**: RV32 can address 4 GB of memory, whereas RV64 can address a much larger space (up to 16 exabytes).
- **Register Width**: In RV32, registers are 32 bits wide; in RV64, they are 64 bits wide.

Practical Implications

- **Performance**: RV32 may be used in applications where 32-bit addressing and operations are sufficient, such as embedded systems and small devices.
- **Complexity and Power Consumption**: RV32 implementations can be simpler and more power-efficient compared to RV64, making them suitable for low-power applications.
- **Software Compatibility**: Software written for RV32 will be different from that written for RV64 due to differences in register width and addressing.

Processing integers

RV32 assembly uses a set of instructions designed to perform arithmetic, logical, and control operations on 32-bit integers. Here's a breakdown of how RV32 handles operations:

Registers

RV32 uses 32 general-purpose registers, each 32 bits wide. These registers are named x0 through x31. Register x0 is hardwired to zero and can be used as a source operand when a zero value is needed.

Basic Integer Operations

Arithmetic Operations
1. **Addition:**

    ADD rd, rs1, rs2
    Adds the values in **rs1** and **rs2**, and stores the result in **rd**.

    ADDI rd, rs1, imm: Adds the value in **rs1** and the immediate value **imm**, storing the result in **rd**.

2. **Subtraction:**

    SUB rd, rs1, rs2: Subtracts the value in **rs2** from **rs1**, and stores the result in **rd**.

Logical Operations
1. **AND**:

   AND rd, rs1, rs2: Performs a bitwise AND on the values in **rs1** and **rs2**, and stores the result in **rd**.

   ANDI rd, rs1, imm: Performs a bitwise AND on the value in **rs1** and the immediate value **imm**, storing the result in **rd**.

2. **OR**:

   OR rd, rs1, rs2: Performs a bitwise OR on the values in **rs1** and **rs2**, and stores the result in **rd**.

   ORI rd, rs1, imm: Performs a bitwise OR on the value in **rs1** and the immediate value **imm**, storing the result in **rd**.

3. **XOR**:

   XOR rd, rs1, rs2: Performs a bitwise XOR on the values in **rs1** and **rs2**, and stores the result in **rd**.

   XORI rd, rs1, imm: Performs a bitwise XOR on the value in **rs1** and the immediate value **imm**, storing the result in **rd**.

Shift Operations
1. **Logical Shift Left**:

   SLL rd, rs1, rs2: Shifts the value in **rs1** left by the number of bits specified in **rs2**, and stores the result in **rd**.

   SLLI rd, rs1, shamt: Shifts the value in **rs1** left by the immediate shift amount **shamt**, and stores the result in **rd**.

2. **Logical Shift Right**:

   SRL rd, rs1, rs2: Shifts the value in **rs1** right by the number of bits specified in **rs2**, and stores the result in **rd**.

SRLI rd, rs1, shamt: Shifts the value in **rs1** right by the immediate shift amount **shamt**, and stores the result in **rd**.

3. **Arithmetic Shift Right**:

   SRA rd, rs1, rs2: Shifts the value in **rs1** right by the number of bits specified in **rs2**, maintaining the sign bit, and stores the result in **rd**.

   SRAI rd, rs1, shamt: Shifts the value in **rs1** right by the immediate shift amount **shamt**, maintaining the sign bit, and stores the result in **rd**.

Control Operations
  1. **Comparison and Branching**:

   BEQ rs1, rs2, offset: Branches to the address **offset** if the values in **rs1** and **rs2** are equal.

   BNE rs1, rs2, offset: Branches to the address **offset** if the values in **rs1** and **rs2** are not equal.

   BLT rs1, rs2, offset: Branches to the address **offset** if the value in **rs1** is less than the value in **rs2**.

   BGE rs1, rs2, offset: Branches to the address **offset** if the value in **rs1** is greater than or equal to the value in **rs2**.

Memory Operations
  • **Load**:

   LW rd, offset(rs1): Loads a 32-bit word from memory at the address [**rs1 + offset**] into **rd**.

   LH rd, offset(rs1): Loads a 16-bit half-word from memory at the address [**rs1 + offset**] into **rd**, sign-extended.

   LHU rd, offset(rs1): Loads a 16-bit half-word from memory at the address [**rs1 + offset**] into **rd**, zero-extended.

LB rd, offset(rs1): Loads an 8-bit byte from memory at the address [**rs1 + offset**] into **rd**, sign-extended.

LBU rd, offset(rs1): Loads an 8-bit byte from memory at the address [**rs1 + offset**] into **rd**, zero-extended.

- **Store**:

    SW rs2, offset(rs1): Stores the 32-bit value in **rs2** to memory at the address [**rs1 + offset**].

    SH rs2, offset(rs1): Stores the lower 16 bits of the value in **rs2** to memory at the address [**rs1 + offset**].

    SB rs2, offset(rs1): Stores the lower 8 bits of the value in **rs2** to memory at the address [**rs1 + offset**].

Example: Adding two numbers

```
addi x1, x0, 10    # x1 = 10
addi x2, x0, 20    # x2 = 20
add  x3, x1, x2    # x3 = x1 + x2 = 30
```

Example: Storing and loading a value

```
addi x4, x0, 100   # x4 = 100
sw   x4, 0(x0)     # Store x4 at address 0
lw   x5, 0(x0)     # Load the value from address 0 into x5
```

Example 1

Below (**Listing 1**) is an example of how we can use RV32 inline assembly code to calculate the sum of the elements of a 10-element integer array. The result is then printed using the **printf** function in the C **main()** procedure.

Listing 1.

```
#include <stdio.h>

int arr[10] = {1, -2, -3, 4, -5, 6, 7, -8, 9, -10};
```

```c
int sum = 0;

int main() {
  asm volatile (
    "li t0, 0\n"          // t0 will hold the sum, initialize to 0
    "li t1, 10\n"         // t1 will hold the loop counter, initialize to 10
    "la t2, arr\n"        // t2 will hold the base address of the array
"loop:\n"
    "lw t3, 0(t2)\n"      // load the current array element into t3
    "add t0, t0, t3\n"    // add the current element to t0
    "addi t2, t2, 4\n"    // move to the next array element (4 bytes)
    "addi t1, t1, -1\n"   // decrement the loop counter
    "bnez t1, loop\n"     // if t1 is not zero, continue the loop
    "la t2, sum\n"        // t2 will hold the address of the sum variable
    "sw t0, 0(t2)\n"      // store the value in t0 in the variable sum
  );

  printf("Sum of array elements: %d\n", sum);
  return 0;
}
```

Below is the explanation of how the assembly code works:

Variable Initialization:
- **t0** is initialized to 0 and will hold the sum.
- **t1** is initialized to 10, representing the number of elements in the array.
- **t2** is loaded with the base address of the array.

Loop:
- **lw t3, 0(t2)**: Load the current element of the array into register **t3**.
- **add t0, t0, t3**: Add the value in **t3** to **t0** (accumulating the sum).
- **addi t2, t2, 4**: Move to the next array element (since each int is 4 bytes).
- **addi t1, t1, -1**: Decrement the loop counter **t1**.
- **bnez t1, loop**: If **t1** is not zero, jump back to the **loop** label.

Output:
- **la t2, sum**: **t2** will hold the address of the **sum** variable.
- **sw t0, 0(t2)**: **t0** will be saved in the variable **sum**.

Example 2

Below is the modified code (**Listing 2**) to calculate the sum of negative elements of a 10-element integer array using RV32 inline assembly. The result is then printed using **printf**.

Listing 2.

```
#include <stdio.h>

int arr[10] = {1, -2, -3, 4, -5, -6, 7, 8, -9, -10};
int sum = 0;

int main() {
    // Inline assembly to calculate the sum of the negative array elements
    asm volatile (
        "li t0, 0\n"              // t0 will hold the sum, initialize to 0
        "li t1, 10\n"             // t1 will hold the loop counter, initialize to 10
        "la t2, arr\n"            // t2 will hold the base address of the array
    "loop:\n"
        "lw t3, 0(t2)\n"          // load the current array element into t3
        "bltz t3, add_neg\n"      // if t3 is negative, jump to add_neg
        "j next\n"                // otherwise, jump to next
    "add_neg:\n"
        "add t0, t0, t3\n"        // add the current element to t0
    "next:\n"
        "addi t2, t2, 4\n"        // move to the next array element (4 bytes)
        "addi t1, t1, -1\n"       // decrement the loop counter
        "bnez t1, loop\n"         // if t1 is not zero, continue the loop
        "la  t2, sum\n"           // load the address of the variable sum in t2
        "sw  t0, 0(t2)\n"         // save t0 in the variable sum
    );
    printf("Sum of negative array elements: %d\n", sum);
    return 0;
}
```

What is changed as compared with the previous code, is the loop:
- **lw t3, 0(t2)**: Loads the current element of the array into register **t3**.
- **bltz t3, add_neg**: If **t3** is negative, jump to the **add_neg** label.

- **j next**: If **t3** is not negative, jump to the **next** label.
- **add_neg**: Add the value in **t3** to **t0** (accumulating the sum of negative elements).
- **addi t2, t2, 4**: Move to the next array element (since each int is 4 bytes).
- **addi t1, t1, -1**: Decrement the loop counter **t1**.
- **bnez t1, loop**: If **t1** is not zero, jump back to the **loop** label.

Example 3

Here's an example of RV32 inline assembly code in C that searches for the maximum value in a 10-element integer array (**Listing 3**):

Listing 3.

```
#include <stdio.h>

int find_max(int *array, int length) {
    int max_value;
    asm volatile (
        "mv t0, %1\n"       // t0 = array
        "lw t1, 0(t0)\n"    // t1 = array[0] (initial max_value)
        "addi t2, t0, 4\n"  // t2 = array + 1
        "li t3, 1\n"        // t3 = 1 (counter)
        "mv t4, %2\n"       // t4 = length

    "1:\n"
        "beq t3, t4, 2f\n"  // if counter == length, jump to end
        "lw t5, 0(t2)\n"    // load array[counter] into t5
        "blt t1, t5, 3f\n"  // if max_value < array[counter], jump to update
                            // max_value
        "j 4f\n"            // else, jump to next iteration

    "3:\n"
        "mv t1, t5\n"       // update max_value

    "4:\n"
```

```
    "addi t2, t2, 4\n"        // increment pointer to next element
    "addi t3, t3, 1\n"        // increment counter
    "j 1b\n"                  // jump back to start of loop

  "2:\n"
    "mv %0, t1\n"             // set max_value to output variable

    : "=r" (max_value)                // output
    : "r" (array), "r" (length)       // inputs
    : "t0", "t1", "t2", "t3", "t4", "t5"  // clobbered registers
  );
  return max_value;
}

int main() {
    int array[10] = {3, 5, 7, 2, 8, -1, 4, 10, 6, 9};
    int max_value = find_max(array, 10);
    printf("Maximum value: %d\n", max_value);
    return 0;
}
```

When begins to run, the code performs setup and initialization:

- **t0** is initialized to point to the start of the array.
- **t1** is set to the first element of the array, serving as the initial maximum value.
- **t2** is set to point to the second element of the array.
- **t3** is used as a counter, starting from 1.
- **t4** is set to the length of the array.

Then the code enters a loop that runs while the counter **t3** is less than the length **t4**. For each iteration, it loads the current array element into **t5**. If the current array element is greater than the current maximum value (**t1**), it updates the maximum value.
The pointer to the next element and the counter are incremented. Once the loop is done, the final maximum value is moved to the output variable.

In the given inline assembly code, labels like **1:\n**, **2:\n**, etc., are used to create local labels within the assembly block. These labels act as targets for jumps and branches, allowing the code to control the flow of execution. Let's break down their roles:

- **1:\n**: This label marks the start of the loop. The code repeatedly jumps back to this label to check the loop condition and iterate through the array.
- **2:\n**: This label marks the end of the loop. When the counter **t3** equals the length **t4**, the code jumps to this label to exit the loop and proceed with the remaining code.
- **3:\n**: This label marks the point where the maximum value is updated. If the current array element (**t5**) is greater than the current maximum value (**t1**), the code jumps to this label to update **t1**.
- **4:\n**: This label is used for the next iteration of the loop. If the current array element is not greater than the current maximum value, the code jumps to this label to increment the pointers and counter and then continue with the next iteration.

The `b` suffix in `1b` and `j 1b` means `backward`, indicating that the jump should go to the most recent previous instance of label 1. Conversely, an `f` suffix (not used in this example but common in other contexts) would mean `forward`, indicating a jump to the next instance of that label.

In the inline assembly code, the expressions **%0, %1**, and **%2** are placeholders for the operands specified in the constraint list. Here's how they map to the parameters and output:
- **%0**: Refers to the output operand, which in this case is **max_value**.
- **%1**: Refers to the first input operand, which is array.
- **%2**: Refers to the second input operand, which is length.

Example 4

It is easily to modify the code from **Example 3** to search for the minimum element of the array. The modified code is shown in **Listing 4**.

Listing 4.

```
#include <stdio.h>

int find_min(int *array, int length) {
    int min_value;
    asm volatile (
```

```
    "mv t0, %1\n"      // t0 = array
    "lw t1, 0(t0)\n"   // t1 = array[0] (initial min_value)
    "addi t2, t0, 4\n" // t2 = array + 1
    "li t3, 1\n"       // t3 = 1 (counter)
    "mv t4, %2\n"      // t4 = length

 "1:\n"
    "beq t3, t4, 2f\n" // if counter == length, jump to end
    "lw t5, 0(t2)\n"   // load array[counter] into t5
    "bgt t1, t5, 3f\n" // if min_value > array[counter], jump to
                       //update min_value
    "j 4f\n"           // else, jump to next iteration

 "3:\n"
    "mv t1, t5\n"      // update min_value

 "4:\n"
    "addi t2, t2, 4\n" // increment pointer to next element
    "addi t3, t3, 1\n" // increment counter
    "j 1b\n"           // jump back to start of loop

 "2:\n"
    "mv %0, t1\n"          // set min_value to output variable

    : "=r" (min_value)                // output
    : "r" (array), "r" (length)       // inputs
    : "t0", "t1", "t2", "t3", "t4", "t5"  // clobbered registers
  );
  return min_value;
}

int main() {
   int array[10] = {3, 5, 7, 2, 8, -1, 4, -10, 6, 9};
   int min_value = find_min(array, 10);
   printf("Minimum value: %d\n", min_value);
   return 0;
}
```

In this code, we defined **min_value** instead of **max_value**, changed the name of the function to **find_min**. The instruction blt t1, t5, 3f

from the previous code (see **Listing 3**) was replaced with the following one

bgt t1, t5, 3f

Example 5

In this example, the inline assembly code (**Listing 5**) calculates the number of elements in the 10-element array that are between 1 and 15 and returns this count to C code.

Listing 5.

```
#include <stdio.h>

int count_elements_in_range(int *array, int length);

int main() {
    int array[10] = {0, 2, -5, 8, -12, 15, 10, -1, 14, 6};
    int count = count_elements_in_range(array, 10);
    printf("Number of elements between 1 and 15: %d\n", count);
    return 0;
}

int count_elements_in_range(int *array, int length) {
    int count = 0;
    asm volatile (
        "li t0, 1\n"          // Load the lower bound 1 into t0
        "li t1, 15\n"         // Load the upper bound 15 into t1
        "mv t2, %1\n"         // Load the address of the array into t2
        "mv t3, %2\n"         // Load the length of the array into t3
        "mv t4, zero\n"       // Initialize count to 0 in t4

    "loop:\n"
        "beqz t3, end\n"      // If length is 0, exit the loop
        "lw t5, 0(t2)\n"      // Load the current element into t5
        "blt t5, t0, skip\n"  // If element < 1, skip incrementing count
```

```
    "bgt t5, t1, skip\n"        // If element > 15, skip incrementing count
    "addi t4, t4, 1\n"          // Increment the count

  "skip:\n"
    "addi t2, t2, 4\n"          // Move to the next array element (assuming 4-
                                //byte integers)
    "addi t3, t3, -1\n"         // Decrement the length
    "j loop\n"                  // Jump back to the beginning of the loop
  "end:\n"
    "mv %0, t4\n"               // Move the count to the output variable

    : "=r" (count)                     // Output
    : "r" (array), "r" (length)        // Inputs
    : "t0", "t1", "t2", "t3", "t4", "t5" // Clobbered registers
  );
  return count;
}
```

Let' analyze the above code.

Setup:

- **li t0, 1**: loads the lower bound 1 into register **t0**.
- **li t1, 15**: loads the upper bound 15 into register **t1**.
- **mv t2, %1**: loads the address of the array into register **t2**.
- **mv t3, %2**: loads the length of the array into register **t3**.
- **mv t4, zero**: initializes the count to 0 in register **t4**.

Loop:

The loop starts with the label **loop**.

- **beqz t3, end**: checks if the length is zero, if so, it jumps to **end**.
- **lw t5, 0(t2)**: loads the current array element into register **t5**.
- **blt t5, t0, skip**: checks if the element is less than 1, if so, it skips the count increment.
- **bgt t5, t1, skip**: checks if the element is greater than 15, if so, it skips the count increment.
- **addi t4, t4, 1**: increments the count.
- **skip**: is the label to skip the count increment.
- **addi t2, t2, 4**: moves to the next array element.
- **addi t3, t3, -1**: decrements the length.
- **j loop**: jumps back to the beginning of the loop.

End:

The label **end** indicates where the loop exits.

- **mv %0, t4**: moves the final count to the output variable count.

Output and Inputs:

- : "=r" (count) specifies that the output variable count is stored in a register.
- : "r" (array), "r" (length) specifies that the inputs array and length are stored in registers.
- : "t0", "t1", "t2", "t3", "t4", "t5" specifies the clobbered registers.

Example 6

The below code (**Listing 6**) inverts each element in the 10-element integer array and stores the inverted values back into the array.

Listing 6.

```
#include <stdio.h>

void invert_elements(int *array, int length);

int main() {
    int array[10] = {0, 2, 5, 8, 12, 15, 17, 1, 14, 6};
    invert_elements(array, 10);
    printf("Inverted array: ");
    for(int i = 0; i < 10; i++) {
        printf("%d ", array[i]);
    }
    printf("\n");
    return 0;
}

void invert_elements(int *array, int length) {
    asm volatile (
        "mv t0, %0\n"          // Load the address of the array into t0
```

```
    "mv t1, %1\n"           // Load the length of the array into t1

  "loop:\n"
      "beqz t1, end\n"       // If length is 0, exit the loop
      "lw t2, 0(t0)\n"       // Load the current element into t2
      "not t2, t2\n"         // Invert the element (bitwise NOT)
      "sw t2, 0(t0)\n"       // Store the inverted element back into the array
      "addi t0, t0, 4\n"     // Move to the next array element (assuming 4-
                             // byte integers)
      "addi t1, t1, -1\n"    // Decrement the length
      "j loop\n"             // Jump back to the beginning of the loop
  "end:\n"

      :                      // No output
      : "r" (array), "r" (length)// Inputs
      : "t0", "t1", "t2"     // Clobbered registers
  );
}
```

Let's analyze the code.

Setup:

- **mv t0, %0**: loads the address of the array into register **t0**.
- **mv t1, %1**: loads the length of the array into register **t1**.

Loop:

The loop starts with the label **loop**.

- **beqz t1, end**: checks if the length is zero, if so, it jumps to **end**.
- **lw t2, 0(t0)**: loads the current array element into register **t2**.
- **not t2, t2**: inverts the element (bitwise NOT).
- **sw t2, 0(t0)**: stores the inverted element back into the array.
- **addi t0, t0, 4**: moves to the next array element.
- **addi t1, t1, -1**: decrements the length.
- **j loop**: jumps back to the beginning of the **loop**.

End:

The label **end** indicates where the loop exits.

Inputs:

: "r" (array), "r" (length) specifies that the inputs array and length are stored in registers.
: "t0", "t1", "t2" specifies the clobbered registers.

Example 7

In this example, the RV32 inline assembly code (**Listing 7**) replaces all negative elements in the array with zero and leaves the rest of the elements unchanged.

Listing 7.

```c
#include <stdio.h>

void replace_negative_elements(int *array, int length);

int main() {
    int array[10] = {0, -2, 5, -8, 12, -15, 17, 1, -14, 6};
    replace_negative_elements(array, 10);
    printf("Array after replacing negative elements: ");
    for(int i = 0; i < 10; i++) {
        printf("%d ", array[i]);
    }
    printf("\n");
    return 0;
}

void replace_negative_elements(int *array, int length) {
    asm volatile (
        "mv t0, %0\n"            // Load the address of the array into t0
        "mv t1, %1\n"            // Load the length of the array into t1

    "loop:\n"
        "beqz t1, end\n"         // If length is 0, exit the loop
        "lw t2, 0(t0)\n"         // Load the current element into t2
        "blt t2, zero, replace\n" // If element is negative, jump to replace
        "j next\n"               // Otherwise, jump to next

    "replace:\n"
```

```
"li t2, 0\n"                    // Load 0 into t2
"sw t2, 0(t0)\n"                // Store 0 into the current element

"next:\n"
    "addi t0, t0, 4\n"          // Move to the next array element (assuming 4-
                                // byte integers)
    "addi t1, t1, -1\n"         // Decrement the length
    "j loop\n"                  // Jump back to the beginning of the loop

"end:\n"

    :                           // No output
    : "r" (array), "r" (length) // Inputs
    : "t0", "t1", "t2"          // Clobbered registers
);
}
```

Explanation
Setup:

- **mv t0, %0:** loads the address of the array into register **t0**.
- **mv t1, %1:** loads the length of the array into register **t1**.

Loop:
The loop starts with the label **loop**.

- **beqz t1, end:** checks if the length is zero, if so, it jumps to **end**.
- **lw t2, 0(t0):** loads the current array element into register **t2**.
- **blt t2, zero, replace:** checks if the element is negative, if so, it jumps to the replace label.
- **j next:** jumps to the **next** label if the element is not negative.

Replace:
The **replace** label is where the negative element is replaced with zero.
li t2, 0: loads 0 into register **t2**.
sw t2, 0(t0): stores 0 into the current array element.

Next:
The **next** label is where the loop continues.

- **addi t0, t0, 4:** moves to the next array element.
- **addi t1, t1, -1:** decrements the length.

- **j loop**: jumps back to the beginning of the loop.

End:

The **end**: label is where the loop exits.

Inputs:
- : "r" (array), "r" (length) specifies that the inputs array and length are stored in registers.
- : "t0", "t1", "t2" specifies the clobbered registers.

Example 8

In this example, the inline assembly code (**Listing 8**) replaces all elements in the 10-element array with their absolute values, ensuring that all elements are non-negative.

Listing 8.

```c
#include <stdio.h>

void replace_with_absolute_values(int *array, int length);

int main() {
    int array[10] = {0, -2, 5, -8, 12, -15, 17, 1, -14, 6};
    replace_with_absolute_values(array, 10);
    printf("Array after replacing with absolute values: ");
    for(int i = 0; i < 10; i++) {
        printf("%d ", array[i]);
    }
    printf("\n");
    return 0;
}

void replace_with_absolute_values(int *array, int length) {
    asm volatile (
        "mv t0, %0\n"        // Load the address of the array into t0
        "mv t1, %1\n"        // Load the length of the array into t1
```

```
"loop:\n"
    "beqz t1, end\n"          // If length is 0, exit the loop
    "lw t2, 0(t0)\n"          // Load the current element into t2
    "bge t2, zero, next\n"    // If element is non-negative, jump to next
    "neg t2, t2\n"            // Negate the element (make it positive)
    "sw t2, 0(t0)\n"          // Store the absolute value back into the array

"next:\n"
    "addi t0, t0, 4\n"        // Move to the next array element (assuming 4-
                             // byte integers)
    "addi t1, t1, -1\n"       // Decrement the length
    "j loop\n"               // Jump back to the beginning of the loop

"end:\n"

    :                        // No output
    : "r" (array), "r" (length)  // Inputs
    : "t0", "t1", "t2"        // Clobbered registers
);
}
```

Explanation
Setup:

- **mv t0, %0**: loads the address of the array into register **t0**.
- **mv t1, %1**: loads the length of the array into register **t1**.

Loop:

- The loop starts with the label **loop**.
- **beqz t1, end**: checks if the length is zero, if so, it jumps to **end**.
- **lw t2, 0(t0)**: loads the current array element into register **t2**.
- **bge t2, zero, next**: checks if the element is non-negative, if so, it jumps to the **next** label.
- **neg t2, t2**: negates the element (makes it positive).
- **sw t2, 0(t0)**: stores the absolute value back into the array.

Next:

- The **next** label is where the loop continues.
- **addi t0, t0, 4**: moves to the next array element.
- **addi t1, t1, -1**: decrements the length.

- **j loop**: jumps back to the beginning of the loop.

End:
- The **end**: label is where the loop exits.

Inputs:
- : "r" (array), "r" (length) specifies that the inputs array and length are stored in registers.
- : "t0", "t1", "t2" specifies the clobbered registers.

Example 9

This code will correctly calculate the square of each element in the source 10-element integer array and store it in the destination array when called from C.
The RV32 assembly procedure (**Listing 9**) calculates the square of each element in a 10-element integer array and stores the result in a new array. This procedure when is called from C code takes two parameters: the addresses of the source and destination arrays.

Listing 9.

```
.section .text
.globl square_array
square_array:
    addi sp, sp, -16      # Adjust stack pointer
    sw ra, 12(sp)         # Save return address
    sw s0, 8(sp)          # Save s0 register
    sw s1, 4(sp)          # Save s1 register
    sw s2, 0(sp)          # Save s2 register

    mv s0, a0             # Load source array address into s0
    mv s1, a1             # Load destination array address into s1

    li s2, 10             # Set loop counter to 10
loop:
    lw t0, 0(s0)          # Load element from source array
    mul t1, t0, t0        # Calculate square of the element
    sw t1, 0(s1)          # Store result in destination array
```

```
addi s0, s0, 4        # Move to next element in source array
addi s1, s1, 4        # Move to next element in destination array
addi s2, s2, -1       # Decrement loop counter
bnez s2, loop         # If counter is not zero, repeat loop

lw ra, 12(sp)         # Restore return address
lw s0, 8(sp)          # Restore s0 register
lw s1, 4(sp)          # Restore s1 register
lw s2, 0(sp)          # Restore s2 register
addi sp, sp, 16       # Restore stack pointer
ret                   # Return to caller
```

Explanation

Procedure Prologue:
- Adjusts the stack pointer to create space for saving registers.
- Saves the return address and callee-saved registers (**s0, s1, s2**).

Loading Parameters:
- **s0** gets the source array address from **a0**.
- **s1** gets the destination array address from **a1**.

Loop:
- Loads an element from the source array into **t0**.
- Squares the element and stores the result in **t1**.
- Stores the squared value in the destination array.
- Increments the pointers for source and destination arrays.
- Decrements the loop counter and checks if it should repeat.

Procedure Epilogue:
- Restores the saved registers and stack pointer.
- Returns to the caller.

Here's an example of how to call this procedure from C code (**Listing 10**).

Listing 10.

#include <stdio.h>

```c
// Declaration of the assembly procedure
void square_array(int *src, int *dst);

int main() {
    int src[10] = {1, -2, -11, 41, -72, 6, 17, 8, 9, -10};
    int dst[10];

    // Call the assembly procedure
    square_array(src, dst);

    // Print the result
    for (int i = 0; i < 10; i++) {
        printf("%d ", dst[i]);
    }
    printf("\n");

    return 0;
}
```

Example 10

In this example, the RV32 assembly procedure (**Listing 11**) provides a basic implementation for calculating the sum of corresponding elements of two 10-element integer arrays and storing the result in a new array.
The assembly procedure takes three parameters: addresses of two input arrays and one output array. The procedure code works as follows:
- Iterates through 10 elements of each array.
- Adds corresponding elements.
- Stores the result in the corresponding element of the output array.

Listing 11.

```
.section text
.global array_sum

array_sum:
    # Prologue
```

```
addi sp, sp, -16   # Allocate space for 4 registers
sw ra, 12(sp)      # Save return address
sw s0, 8(sp)       # Save s0 (array1)
sw s1, 4(sp)       # Save s1 (array2)
sw s2, 0(sp)       # Save s2 (result)

# Load arguments into registers
mv s0, a0      # s0 = array1 address
mv s1, a1      # s1 = array2 address
mv s2, a2      # s2 = result array address

# Initialize loop counter
li t0, 10      # t0 = loop counter

loop:
# Load elements from arrays
lw t1, 0(s0)    # t1 = element from array1
lw t2, 0(s1)    # t2 = element from array2

# Calculate sum
add t3, t1, t2  # t3 = sum of elements

# Store result in output array
sw t3, 0(s2)    # Store sum in result array

# Increment pointers
addi s0, s0, 4  # Increment array1 pointer
addi s1, s1, 4  # Increment array2 pointer
addi s2, s2, 4  # Increment result array pointer

# Decrement loop counter
addi t0, t0, -1  # Decrement loop counter

bne t0, zero, loop # Continue loop if t0 != 0

# Epilogue
lw ra, 12(sp)    # Restore return address
lw s0, 8(sp)     # Restore s0
lw s1, 4(sp)     # Restore s1
lw s2, 0(sp)     # Restore s2
```

```
addi sp, sp, 16  # Deallocate stack space
ret              # Return
```

Explanation:

1. **Prologue:** Allocates space on the stack for saved registers, saves return address and used registers.
2. **Load arguments:** Loads the addresses of the input and output arrays into registers **s0, s1,** and **s2.**
3. **Initialize loop counter:** Sets register **t0** to 10 for the loop counter.
4. **Loop:**
   - Loads elements from **array1** and **array2** into registers **t1** and **t2.**
   - Calculates the sum and stores it in **t3.**
   - Stores the sum in the current position of the result array.
   - Increments pointers for all three arrays.
   - Decrements the loop counter.
   - Checks if the loop counter is zero and jumps back to the loop if not.
5. **Epilogue:** Restores saved registers and deallocates stack space before returning.

The C code that calls the above procedure is shown in **Listing 12.**

Listing 12.

```c
#include <stdio.h>

extern void array_sum(int *arr1, int *arr2, int *result);

int main() {
  int arr1[10] = {1, 2, 3, 4, 5, 6, 7, 8, 9, 10};
  int arr2[10] = {-10, -9, -8, -7, -6, -5, -4, -3, -2, -1};
  int result[10];

  array_sum(arr1, arr2, result);

  // Print the result array (for testing)
  for (int i = 0; i < 10; i++) {
    printf("%d ", result[i]);
  }
}
```

```
printf("\n");

return 0;
}
```

Note:

- This code assumes that the arrays are 32-bit integer arrays.
- The code uses standard calling conventions for RV32.
- The code can be optimized further by using different registers or instruction sequences.
- For larger arrays, consider using a different loop structure or unrolling the loop for performance improvement.

Example 11

In this example, the RV32 assembly procedure (**Listing 13**) provides a basic implementation for calculating the sum of corresponding elements of two 10-element integer arrays and storing the positive resulting values in a new array.

The assembly procedure takes three parameters: addresses of two input arrays and one output array. The procedure code works as follows:

- Calculate the sum of corresponding elements from two 10-element integer arrays.
- Only store positive results in a new array.

This procedure maintains the same function signature (see **Example 10**) with three parameters.

Listing 13.

```
.section text
.global array_sum_positive

array_sum_positive:
  # Prologue
    addi sp, sp, -16 # Allocate space for 4 registers
```

```
    sw ra, 12(sp)    # Save return address
    sw s0, 8(sp)     # Save s0 (array1)
    sw s1, 4(sp)     # Save s1 (array2)
    sw s2, 0(sp)     # Save s2 (result)

  # Load arguments into registers
    mv s0, a0        # s0 = array1 address
    mv s1, a1        # s1 = array2 address
    mv s2, a2        # s2 = result array address

  # Initialize loop counter and result array index
    li t0, 10        # t0 = loop counter
    li t4, 0         # t4 = index for result array

loop:
    # Load elements from arrays
    lw t1, 0(s0)     # t1 = element from array1
    lw t2, 0(s1)     # t2 = element from array2

  # Calculate sum
    add t3, t1, t2   # t3 = sum of elements

    # Check if sum is positive
    blt t3, zero, skip_store

    # Store positive result in output array
    sw t3, 0(s2)     # Store sum in result array
    addi s2, s2, 4   # Increment result array pointer
    addi t4, t4, 1   # Increment result array index

skip_store:
    # Increment pointers for input arrays
    addi s0, s0, 4   # Increment array1 pointer
    addi s1, s1, 4   # Increment array2 pointer

    # Decrement loop counter
    addi t0, t0, -1  # Decrement loop counter
    bne t0, zero, loop # Continue loop if t0 != 0

    # Epilogue
```

```
lw ra, 12(sp)    # Restore return address
lw s0, 8(sp)     # Restore s0
lw s1, 4(sp)     # Restore s1
lw s2, 0(sp)     # Restore s2
addi sp, sp, 16  # Deallocate stack space
ret              # Return
```

Explanation of Changes

- Added a new register **t4** to keep track of the index for the result array.
- Introduced a **skip_store** label to avoid storing negative values.
- Conditional branch `blt t3, zero`, **skip_store** checks if the sum is less than zero.
- If the sum is positive, it stores the result in the result array and increments the result array index.

This modified code calculates the sum of corresponding elements and stores only positive results in the new array.

The C code that calls the **array_sum_positive** function is shown in **Listing 14**.

Listing 14.

```c
#include <stdio.h>

extern void array_sum_positive(int *arr1, int *arr2, int *result);

int main() {
  int arr1[10] = {1, 12, 3, 14, 5, 6, -7, 8, 9, -10};
  int arr2[10] = {-10, -9, -8, -7, -6, -5, -4, -3, -2, -1};
  int result[10];

  array_sum_positive(arr1, arr2, result);

  // Print the result array (for testing)
  for (int i = 0; i < 10; i++) {
    printf("%d ", result[i]);
  }
  printf("\n");
```

```
  return 0;
}
```

The C code for calling this function remains the same as in the previous example, except for changing the function name to **array_sum_positive**.

Example 12

In this example, the inline assembly procedure sorts the elements of the array in descending order using a bubble sort (**Listing 15**).

Listing 15.

```
#include <stdio.h>

void sort_descending(int *array, int length);

int main() {
    int array[10] = {0, -2, 5, -8, 12, -15, 17, 1, -14, 6};
    sort_descending(array, 10);
    printf("Array after sorting in descending order: ");
    for(int i = 0; i < 10; i++) {
        printf("%d ", array[i]);
    }
    printf("\n");
    return 0;
}

void sort_descending(int *array, int length) {
    asm volatile (
        "mv t0, %0\n"          // Load the address of the array into t0
        "mv t1, %1\n"          // Load the length of the array into t1
        "addi t1, t1, -1\n"    // t1 = length - 1

    "outer_loop:\n"
        "beqz t1, end\n"       // If t1 is 0, exit the outer loop
        "mv t2, t1\n"          // t2 = t1 (inner loop counter)

    "inner_loop:\n"
```

```
"addi t2, t2, -1\n"       // Decrement t2
"bltz t2, next_outer\n"   // If t2 < 0, go to next outer loop iteration
"slli t3, t2, 2\n"        // t3 = t2 * 4 (offset for 4-byte integers)
"add t4, t0, t3\n"        // t4 = array base address + offset

"lw t5, 0(t4)\n"                // Load array[t4] into t5
"lw t6, 4(t4)\n"                // Load array[t4 + 1] into t6
"bge t5, t6, inner_loop\n" // If array[t4] >= array[t4 + 1], continue
                               // inner loop

"sw t6, 0(t4)\n"          // Swap elements: store array[t4 + 1] into
                          // array[t4]
"sw t5, 4(t4)\n"          // Swap elements: store array[t4] into array[t4 + 1]

"j inner_loop\n"          // Jump to the start of the inner loop

"next_outer:\n"
    "addi t1, t1, -1\n"        // Decrement outer loop counter
    "j outer_loop\n"          // Jump to the start of the outer loop

"end:\n"

    :                 // No output
    : "r" (array), "r" (length)// Inputs
    : "t0", "t1", "t2", "t3", "t4", "t5", "t6" // Clobbered registers
);
}
```

Explanation
Setup:

- **mv t0, %0**: loads the address of the array into register **t0**.
- **mv t1, %1**: loads the length of the array into register **t1**.
- **addi t1, t1, -1**: decrements the length by 1, to use as the outer loop counter.

Outer Loop:
The outer loop starts with the label **outer_loop:**

- **beqz t1, end**: checks if the length is zero, if so, it jumps to **end**.
- **mv t2, t1**: sets the inner loop counter **t2** to the value of the outer loop counter **t1**.

35

Inner Loop:

The inner loop starts with the label **inner_loop**:

- **addi t2, t2, -1**: decrements the inner loop counter **t2**.
- **bltz t2, next_outer**: checks if **t2** is less than zero, if so, it jumps to **next_outer** to start the next iteration of the outer loop.
- **slli t3, t2, 2**: calculates the offset for 4-byte integers by multiplying **t2** by 4.
- **add t4, t0, t3**: calculates the address of the current element in the array.

Comparison and Swap:

- **lw t5, 0(t4)**: loads the current element array[**t4**] into **t5**.
- **lw t6, 4(t4)**: loads the next element array[**t4** + 1] into **t6**.
- **bge t5, t6, inner_loop**: checks if array[**t4**] is greater than or equal to array[**t4** + 1], if so, it jumps to the start of the inner loop.
- **sw t6, 0(t4)**: swaps the elements by storing array[**t4** + 1] into array[**t4**].
- **sw t5, 4(t4)**: swaps the elements by storing array[**t4**] into array[**t4** + 1].

Next Iteration:

- **j inner_loop**: jumps to the start of the inner loop.
- The **next_outer**: label is where the outer loop continues.
- **addi t1, t1, -1**: decrements the outer loop counter.
- **j outer_loop**: jumps to the start of the outer loop.

End:

The **end**: label is where the outer loop exits.

Inputs and Clobbered Registers:

- : "r" (array), "r" (length) specifies that the inputs array and length are stored in registers.
- : "t0", "t1", "t2", "t3", "t4", "t5", "t6" specifies the clobbered registers.

Example 13

In this example, the RV32 inline assembly code (**Listing 16**) sorts the elements in an array in ascending order using a bubble sort algorithm.

Listing 16.

```c
#include <stdio.h>

void sort_ascending(int *array, int length);

int main() {
    int array[10] = {0, -2, 5, -8, 12, -15, 17, 1, -14, 6};
    sort_ascending(array, 10);
    printf("Array after sorting in ascending order: ");
    for(int i = 0; i < 10; i++) {
        printf("%d ", array[i]);
    }
    printf("\n");
    return 0;
}

void sort_ascending(int *array, int length) {
    asm volatile (
        "mv t0, %0\n"          // Load the address of the array into t0
        "mv t1, %1\n"          // Load the length of the array into t1
        "addi t1, t1, -1\n"    // t1 = length - 1

      "outer_loop:\n"
        "beqz t1, end\n"       // If t1 is 0, exit the outer loop
        "mv t2, zero\n"        // t2 = 0 (inner loop counter)

      "inner_loop:\n"
        "slli t3, t2, 2\n"     // t3 = t2 * 4 (offset for 4-byte integers)
        "add t4, t0, t3\n"     // t4 = array base address + offset

        "lw t5, 0(t4)\n"       // Load array[t4] into t5
        "lw t6, 4(t4)\n"       // Load array[t4 + 1] into t6
        "ble t5, t6, no_swap\n"  // If array[t4] <= array[t4 + 1], continue
                               //    inner loop

        // Swap elements: store array[t4 + 1] into array[t2]
```

```
    "sw t6, 0(t4)\n"
    // Swap elements: store array[t4] into array[t4 + 1]
    "sw t5, 4(t4)\n"

"no_swap:\n"
    "addi t2, t2, 1\n"        // Increment t2
    "blt t2, t1, inner_loop\n" // If t2 < t1, continue inner loop

    "addi t1, t1, -1\n"       // Decrement outer loop counter
    "j outer_loop\n"          // Jump to the start of the outer loop

"end:\n"

    :                         // No output
    : "r" (array), "r" (length)// Inputs
    : "t0", "t1", "t2", "t3", "t4", "t5", "t6" // Clobbered registers
);
}
```

Explanation

Setup:
- **mv t0, %0**: loads the address of the array into register **t0**.
- **mv t1, %1**: loads the length of the array into register **t1**.
- **addi t1, t1, -1**: decrements the length by 1, to use as the outer loop counter.

Outer Loop:
The outer loop starts with the label **outer_loop**:
- **beqz t1, end**: checks if the length is zero, if so, it jumps to **end**.
- **mv t2, zero**: sets the inner loop counter **t2** to zero.

Inner Loop:
The inner loop starts with the label **inner_loop**:
- **slli t3, t2, 2**: calculates the offset for 4-byte integers by multiplying **t2** by 4.
- **add t4, t0, t3**: calculates the address of the current element in the array.

Comparison and Swap:

38

- **lw t5, 0(t4)**: loads the current element array[t4] into **t5**.
- **lw t6, 4(t4)**: loads the next element array[t4 + 1] into **t6**.
- **ble t5, t6, no_swap**: checks if array[t4] is less than or equal to array[t4 + 1], if so, it jumps to **no_swap**.
- Swaps the elements if array[t4] is greater than array[t4 + 1]:
  - **sw t6, 0(t4)**: stores array[t4 + 1] into array[t4].
  - **sw t5, 4(t4)**: stores array[t4] into array[t4 + 1].

Next Iteration:
- **no_swap**: label for no swapping case.
- **addi t2, t2, 1**: increments the inner loop counter.
- **blt t2, t1, inner_loop**: checks if **t2** is less than **t1**, if so, it jumps to the start of the inner loop.
- **addi t1, t1, -1**: decrements the outer loop counter.
- **j outer_loop**: jumps to the start of the outer loop.

End:
The **end**: label is where the outer loop exits.

Inputs and Clobbered Registers:
- : "r" (array), "r" (length) specifies that the inputs array and length are stored in registers.
- : "t0", "t1", "t2", "t3", "t4", "t5", "t6" specifies the clobbered registers.

Example 14

In this example, complete C code with an RV32 inline assembly procedure (**Listing 17**) reverses the order of integers in a 10-element array:

Listing 17.

```
#include <stdio.h>

void reverse_array(int *arr) {
    asm volatile (
        "addi t0, zero, 9\n"    // t0 = 9 (last index)
```

39

```
    "addi t1, zero, 0\n"      //t1 = 0 (first index)
    "add t2, %0, zero\n"      //t2 = arr (start of array)
    "slli t3, t0, 2\n"        //t3 = 9 * 4 = 36 (offset to last element)
    "add t3, t2, t3\n"        // t3 = arr + 36 (address of last element)
  "loop:\n"
    "bge t1, t0, end\n"       // if t1 >= t0, exit loop
    "lw t4, 0(t2)\n"          // load arr[t1]
    "lw t5, 0(t3)\n"          // load arr[t0]
    "sw t5, 0(t2)\n"          // store t5 to arr[t1]
    "sw t4, 0(t3)\n"          // store t4 to arr[t0]
    "addi t2, t2, 4\n"        // move t2 to next element
    "addi t3, t3, -4\n"       // move t3 to previous element
    "addi t1, t1, 1\n"        // increment t1
    "addi t0, t0, -1\n"       // decrement t0
    "j loop\n"                // repeat loop
  "end:\n"

    :
    : "r" (arr)
    : "t0", "t1", "t2", "t3", "t4", "t5"
  );
}

void print_array(int *arr, int size) {
  for (int i = 0; i < size; i++) {
    printf("%d ", arr[i]);
  }
  printf("\n");
}

int main() {
  int arr[10] = {1, 2, 3, 4, 5, 6, 7, 8, 9, 10};
  int size = sizeof(arr) / sizeof(arr[0]);

  printf("Original array: ");
  print_array(arr, size);
  reverse_array(arr);
  printf("Reversed array: ");
  print_array(arr, size);
  return 0;
}
```

This code does the following:

2. It includes the necessary header file (stdio.h) for input/output operations.
3. It defines the **reverse_array** function containing the RV32 inline assembly code we created earlier.
4. It includes a helper function **print_array** to display the contents of an array.
5. In the **main** function:
   - It initializes a 10-element integer array with values 1 through 10.
   - It prints the original array.
   - It calls the **reverse_array** function to reverse the array in place.
   - It prints the reversed array.

When compiled and run on a RISC-V system with the appropriate compiler (e.g., gcc with RISC-V support), this program will reverse the array using the inline assembly code and display both the original and reversed arrays.

Example 15

Below is an example of RV32 inline assembly code (**Listing 18**) to concatenate two 5-element integer arrays into a single 10-element integer array.

Listing 18.

```
#include <stdio.h>

void concatenate_arrays(int* array1, int* array2, int* result);

int main() {
    int array1[5] = {0, -2, 5, -8, 12};
    int array2[5] = {-15, 17, 1, -14, 6};
    int result[10];

    concatenate_arrays(array1, array2, result);
    printf("Resulting array after concatenating: ");
    for(int i = 0; i < 10; i++) {
```

41

```c
        printf("%d ", result[i]);
    }
    printf("\n");
    return 0;
}

void concatenate_arrays(int* array1, int* array2, int* result) {
    asm volatile (
        // Copy elements from array1 to result
        "li t0, 0\n"              // t0 = 0 (index)
    "1:\n"
        "lw t1, 0(%0)\n"          // t1 = array1[t0]
        "sw t1, 0(%2)\n"          // result[t0] = t1
        "addi %0, %0, 4\n"        // increment array1 pointer
        "addi %2, %2, 4\n"        // increment result pointer
        "addi t0, t0, 1\n"        // t0++
        "li t2, 5\n"              // t2 = 5
        "bne t0, t2, 1b\n"        // if t0 != 5, loop

        // Copy elements from array2 to result
        "li t0, 0\n"              // t0 = 0 (index)
    "2:\n"
        "lw t1, 0(%1)\n"          // t1 = array2[t0]
        "sw t1, 0(%2)\n"          // result[5 + t0] = t1
        "addi %1, %1, 4\n"        // increment array2 pointer
        "addi %2, %2, 4\n"        // increment result pointer
        "addi t0, t0, 1\n"        // t0++
        "li t2, 5\n"              // t2 = 5
        "bne t0, t2, 2b\n"        // if t0 != 5, loop
        :
        : "r"(array1), "r"(array2), "r"(result)
        : "t0", "t1", "t2"
    );
}
```

Explanation

First Loop (Copy from array1 to result):
- **t0** is used as the index initialized to 0.
- Loop label `1` is defined to start copying elements.

- Load the element from **array1** indexed by **t0** into **t1**.
- Store the element in result at the corresponding position.
- Increment the **array1** and **result** pointers by 4 (size of an integer).
- Increment **t0**.
- Loop until **t0** equals 5.

Second Loop (Copy from array2 to result):
- Similar to the first loop but starts copying elements from **array2**.
- The **result** pointer is already at the position after the first 5 elements from **array1**.
- Loop label `2` is defined to start copying elements.
- Process is the same as the first loop.

Example 16

Here is an example of an RV32 inline assembly procedure (**Listing 19**) that compares two 10-element integer arrays and returns the number of unmatched elements to C code.

Listing 19.

```
#include <stdio.h>

int compare_arrays(int* array1, int* array2) {
    int unmatched_count = 0;
    asm volatile (
        "li t0, 0\n"            // t0 = 0 (index)
        "li t1, 0\n"            // t1 = 0 (unmatched count)
        "li t2, 10\n"          // t2 = 10 (number of elements)
    "1:\n"
        "beq t0, t2, 2f\n"     // if t0 == 10, exit loop
        "lw t3, 0(%1)\n"       // t3 = array1[t0]
        "lw t4, 0(%2)\n"       // t4 = array2[t0]
        "bne t3, t4, 3f\n"     // if array1[t0] != array2[t0], increment
                               //unmatched count
        "j 4f\n"               // jump to increment pointers
    "3:\n"
```

```
    "addi t1, t1, 1\n"          // t1++
"4:\n"
    "addi %1, %1, 4\n"          // increment array1 pointer
    "addi %2, %2, 4\n"          // increment array2 pointer
    "addi t0, t0, 1\n"          // t0++
    "j 1b\n"                     // jump to start of loop
"2:\n"
    "sw t1, %0\n"                // store unmatched count to output variable
    : "=m"(unmatched_count)
    : "r"(array1), "r"(array2)
    : "t0", "t1", "t2", "t3", "t4"
);
    return unmatched_count;
}

int main() {
    int array1[10] = {1, 2, 3, 14, 5, 6, 7, 8, 9, 10};
    int array2[10] = {1, 2, 3, 4, -15, 6, 7, -11, 0, 10};

    int unmatched = compare_arrays(array1, array2);
    printf("Number of unmatched elements: %d\n", unmatched);

    return 0;
}
```

Explanation

Initialization:
- **t0** is used as the index and initialized to 0.
- **t1** is used to count unmatched elements and initialized to 0.
- **t2** is set to 10, the number of elements in the arrays.

Loop (label `1`):
- The loop checks if the index **t0** has reached 10; if so, it exits the loop (label `2`).
- Loads the current elements from **array1** and **array2** into **t3** and **t4**, respectively.
- Compares the elements:

- If they are not equal, it increments the unmatched count (**t1**) and jumps to label `4` to increment pointers.
- If they are equal, it jumps directly to label `4` to increment pointers.
- Increments the pointers of **array1** and **array2** and the index **t0**.
- Jumps back to the start of the loop (label `1`).

End of Loop (label `2`**):**
Stores the unmatched count (**t1**) into the output variable **unmatched_count**.

Example 17

In this example, the RV32 inline assembly procedure (**Listing 20**) compares two 10-element integer arrays. If both arrays match, the procedure returns 1 to the C main procedure; otherwise, it returns 0.

Listing 20.

```
#include <stdio.h>

int compare_arrays(int *a, int *b) {
    int result;
    asm volatile (
        "li t0, 0\n"                  // Initialize index t0 to 0
        "li t1, 1\n"                  // Initialize result to 1 (true)
        "li t2, 10\n"                 // Set loop limit to 10
    "loop:\n"
        "beq t0, t2, end\n"           // If t0 == 10, exit loop
        "lw t3, 0(%[a])\n"            // Load a[t0] into t3
        "lw t4, 0(%[b])\n"            // Load b[t0] into t4
        "bne t3, t4, mismatch\n"      // If a[t0] != b[t0], go to mismatch
        "addi t0, t0, 1\n"            // Increment index t0
        "addi %[a], %[a], 4\n"        // Move to the next element in a
        "addi %[b], %[b], 4\n"        // Move to the next element in b
        "j loop\n"                    // Jump to the beginning of the loop
    "mismatch:\n"
        "li t1, 0\n"                  // Set result to 0 (false)
    "end:\n"
```

```
        "mv %[result], t1\n"        // Move result into output variable
        : [result] "=r" (result)
        : [a] "r" (a), [b] "r" (b)
        : "t0", "t1", "t2", "t3", "t4"
    );

    return result;
}

int main() {
    int array1[10] = {0, 1, 2, 3, 4, 5, 6, 7, 8, 9};
    int array2[10] = {0, 1, 2, 3, 4, 5, 6, 7, 8, 9};
    int result = compare_arrays(array1, array2);

    if (result == 1) {
        printf("Arrays match.\n");
    } else {
        printf("Arrays do not match.\n");
    }

    return 0;
}
```

Explanation

The inline assembly code compares the elements of two arrays, `a` and `b`, each of size 10.

Registers **t0** to **t4** are used for looping and comparison:

- **t0** is the loop index.
- **t1** stores the result (initially set to 1, indicating arrays match).
- **t2** is the loop limit (10).
- **t3** and **t4** are used to load the current elements of arrays `a` and `b`.
- The loop runs from 0 to 9, comparing corresponding elements of the two arrays.
- If a mismatch is found, **t1** is set to 0, and the loop terminates.
- After the loop, the result is stored in the **result** variable, which is then returned to the calling C function.

Example 18

Below (**Listing 21**) is an RV32 inline assembly procedure to compare two 10-element integer arrays and write the indexes of unmatched elements in a third array.

Listing 21.

```
#include <stdio.h>

void compare_arrays(const int* arr1, const int* arr2, int* result) {
    asm volatile (
        "li t0, 0\n"                 // Initialize index to 0
        "li t1, 0\n"                 // Initialize result index to 0
    "compare_loop:\n"
        "lw t2, 0(%0)\n"             // Load element from arr1
        "lw t3, 0(%1)\n"             // Load element from arr2
        "beq t2, t3, skip_store\n"   // If elements are equal, skip storing index

        "sw t0, 0(%2)\n"             // Store index to result array
        "addi %2, %2, 4\n"           // Increment result array pointer
        "addi t1, t1, 1\n"           // Increment result index

    "skip_store:\n"
        "addi %0, %0, 4\n"           // Increment arr1 pointer
        "addi %1, %1, 4\n"           // Increment arr2 pointer
        "addi t0, t0, 1\n"           // Increment index
        "li t4, 10\n"                // Load array length (10 elements)
        "bne t0, t4, compare_loop"   // If index < 10, repeat

        : // No output operands
        : "r"(arr1), "r"(arr2), "r"(result) // Input operands
        : "t0", "t1", "t2", "t3", "t4" // Clobbered registers
    );
}

int main() {
    const int arr1[10] = {1, 2, 3, 4, 5, 6, 7, 8, 9, 10};
    const int arr2[10] = {1, 2, 0, 4, 5, 0, 7, 8, 9, 0};
```

```c
int result[10] = {0}; // Initialize result array to zero

compare_arrays(arr1, arr2, result);

// Print the indexes of unmatched elements
for (int i = 0; i < 10; i++) {
    if (result[i] != 0) {
        printf("Unmatched index: %d\n", result[i]);
    }
}

return 0;
}
```

Explanation

Initialization:
- **t0** is used as the index counter for the arrays.
- **t1** is used as the index counter for the result array.

Loop (compare_loop):
- Load elements from both arrays.
- Compare the elements using the **beq** instruction.
- If elements are not equal, store the current index in the result array.
- Increment pointers and indices accordingly.
- Check if all elements have been processed using **bne**.

Function and Main:
- The function **compare_arrays** takes pointers to two input arrays (**arr1** and **arr2**) and a result array (**result**).
- The main function initializes the arrays and calls **compare_arrays**. It then prints the indexes of unmatched elements.

Example 19

This example (**Listing 22**) demonstrates how to integrate inline assembly within C to perform element-wise comparison and replacement in two arrays, which is typical in embedded or performance-critical applications.

Listing 22.

```c
#include <stdio.h>

void compare_and_replace(int *arr1, int *arr2, int size) {
    asm volatile (
        "li t0, 0\n"                    // Initialize t0 to 0 (loop index)
    "1:\n"
        "beq t0, %[size], 2f\n"         // If t0 == size, exit loop
        "slli t1, t0, 2\n"             // t1 = t0 * 4 (byte offset)
        "add t2, %[arr1], t1\n"        // t2 = arr1 + t1
        "add t3, %[arr2], t1\n"        // t3 = arr2 + t1
        "lw t4, 0(t2)\n"               // Load arr1[t0] into t4
        "lw t5, 0(t3)\n"               // Load arr2[t0] into t5
        "beq t4, t5, 3f\n"             // If arr1[t0] == arr2[t0], skip
                                       //replacement
        "sw zero, 0(t2)\n"             // Set arr1[t0] to 0
        "sw zero, 0(t3)\n"             // Set arr2[t0] to 0
    "3:\n"
        "addi t0, t0, 1\n"             // Increment loop index
        "j 1b\n"                       // Jump back to start of loop
    "2:\n"

        : [arr1] "r" (arr1), [arr2] "r" (arr2), [size] "r" (size)
        : "t0", "t1", "t2", "t3", "t4", "t5"
    );
}

int main() {
    int arr1[10] = {1, 2, 3, 4, 5, 6, 7, 8, 9, 10};
    int arr2[10] = {1, 2, 0, 4, 0, 6, 7, 0, 9, 0};

    compare_and_replace(arr1, arr2, 10);

    printf("Array 1: ");
    for(int i = 0; i < 10; i++) {
```

```c
        printf("%d ", arr1[i]);
    }
    printf("\n");

    printf("Array 2: ");
    for(int i = 0; i < 10; i++) {
        printf("%d ", arr2[i]);
    }
    printf("\n");

    return 0;
}
```

Explanation
Setup:

- **t0** is used as the loop index.
- **t1** calculates the byte offset for array indexing (each integer is 4 bytes).
- **t2** and **t3** hold the addresses of the current elements of **arr1** and **arr2**.

Loop (1: to 2:):

- The loop iterates from 0 to size - 1 (10 in this case).
- For each element, it loads the elements from both arrays into **t4** and **t5**.
- If the elements are not equal, both elements are set to 0.

Termination:

The loop continues until **t0** equals the size of the arrays.

Example 20

This example (**Listing 23**) demonstrates how to properly convert unsigned bytes to unsigned integers in an array using inline assembly, ensuring that the values are accurately represented.

Listing 23.

#include <stdio.h>

```c
void convert_bytes_to_uints(unsigned char *byte_array, unsigned int
*int_array, int size) {
    asm volatile (
        "li t0, 0\n"                    // Initialize t0 to 0 (loop index)
    "1:\n"
        "beq t0, %[size], 2f\n"         // If t0 == size, exit loop
        "slli t1, t0, 2\n"              // t1 = t0 * 4 (byte offset for int array)
        "add t2, %[byte_array], t0\n"   // t2 = byte_array + t0
        "add t3, %[int_array], t1\n"    // t3 = int_array + t1
        "lbu t4, 0(t2)\n"               // Load byte_array[t0] into t4 as an
                                        //unsigned byte
        "sw t4, 0(t3)\n"                // Store t4 into int_array[t0]
        "addi t0, t0, 1\n"              // Increment loop index
        "j 1b\n"                        // Jump back to start of loop
    "2:\n"

        : [byte_array] "r" (byte_array), [int_array] "r" (int_array), [size] "r" (size)
        : "t0", "t1", "t2", "t3", "t4"
    );
}

int main() {
    unsigned char byte_array[10] = {1, 255, 3, 4, 95, 6, 17, 8, 9, 10};
    unsigned int int_array[10] = {0};

    convert_bytes_to_uints(byte_array, int_array, 10);

    printf("Converted Integer Array: ");
    for(int i = 0; i < 10; i++) {
        printf("%u ", int_array[i]);
    }
    printf("\n");

    return 0;
}
```

Explanation

Setup:

- **t0** is used as the loop index.
- **t1** calculates the byte offset for the integer array (each integer is 4 bytes).
- **t2** and **t3** hold the addresses of the current elements of **byte_array** and **int_array**.

Loop (`1`: to `2`:):
- The loop iterates from 0 to size - 1 (10 in this case).
- For each element, it loads the unsigned byte from **byte_array** into **t4** using the **lbu** instruction.
- It then stores the value of **t4** into the corresponding position in **int_array**.

Termination:
The loop continues until **t0** equals the size of the arrays.

Example 21

In this example (**Listing 24**), the byte values from 0 to 255 in a 10-element byte array will be correctly mapped to the range [-128, 127]. Running this program should yield the expected results, where a byte value of 0 becomes -128, a byte value of 255 becomes 127, and intermediate values are mapped accordingly.

Listing 24.

```
#include <stdio.h>
#include <stdint.h>

void map_range(uint8_t *input, int32_t *output, int length) {
    asm volatile (
        "li t0, 128\n\t"          // Load 128 into t0
        "li t1, 0\n\t"            // Initialize t1 to 0 (index)
     "1:\n\t"
        "lbu t2, 0(%[in])\n\t"    // Load unsigned byte from input array
        "sub t2, t2, t0\n\t"      // Subtract 128 to map the range
        "sw t2, 0(%[out])\n\t"    // Store the result in output array
        "addi %[in], %[in], 1\n\t" // Increment input pointer
```

```
        "addi %[out], %[out], 4\n\t"   // Increment output pointer
        "addi t1, t1, 1\n\t"           // Increment index
        "blt t1, %[len], 1b\n\t"       // If t1 < length, loop
        : [in] "+r" (input), [out] "+r" (output)
        : [len] "r" (length)
        : "t0", "t1", "t2"
    );
}

int main() {
    uint8_t input[10] = {10, 25, 0, 175, 100, 39, 255, 67, 200, 6};
    int32_t output[10];

    map_range(input, output, 10);

    for(int i = 0; i < 10; i++) {
        printf("output[%d] = %d\n", i, output[i]);
    }
    return 0;
}
```

Explanation:

- **Input and Output Arrays**: The input array is an array of 10 bytes, and the output array is an array of 10 integers.
- **Inline Assembly Block**: The inline assembly block performs the following steps:
  - **li t0, 128**: Load the value 128 into register **t0**.
  - **li t1, 0**: Initialize the index **t1** to 0.
  - Loop:
    - **lbu t2, 0(%[in])**: Load the byte as an unsigned value, ensuring it correctly represents values from 0 to 255.
    - **sub t2, t2, t0**: Subtract 128 from **t2** to map the value to the range [-128, 127].
    - **sw t2, 0(%[out])**: Store the result in the output array.
    - **addi %[in], %[in], 1**: Increment the input pointer to the next byte.
    - **addi %[out], %[out], 4**: Increment the output pointer to the next integer.

- **addi t1, t1, 1**: Increment the index.
  - **blt t1, %[len], 1b**: Loop back if the index is less than the length.
- **Registers: t0, t1**, and **t2** are temporary registers used within the assembly block.
- **Pointer Updates**: input and output pointers are updated within the loop.

Example 22

Below (**Listing 25**) is the RV32 assembly procedure **reverse_bytes** that reverses the order of bytes in a 32-bit unsigned integer.

Listing 25.

```
.section .text
.global reverse_bytes
reverse_bytes:
    li t0, 0xFF          # Load mask for extracting bytes
    and t1, a0, t0       # Extract the lowest byte
    sll t1, t1, 24       # Shift it to the highest byte position

    srl t2, a0, 8        # Shift right to bring the second byte to the lowest
                         #position
    and t2, t2, t0       # Extract the second byte
    sll t2, t2, 16       # Shift it to the second highest byte position

    srl t3, a0, 16       # Shift right to bring the third byte to the lowest
                         # position
    and t3, t3, t0       # Extract the third byte
    sll t3, t3, 8        # Shift it to the third highest byte position

    srl t4, a0, 24       # Shift right to bring the highest byte to the lowest
                         # position
    and t4, t4, t0       # Extract the highest byte

    or t1, t1, t2        # Combine the highest and second highest byte
    or t1, t1, t3        # Combine the result with the third byte
```

```
    or a0, t1, t4        # Combine the result with the lowest byte
    ret                  # Return with the reversed bytes in a0
```

Here's a brief explanation of how this procedure works:
1. The input integer is in **a0**.
2. Mask out each byte using 0xFF and place them in the correct position by shifting.
3. Combine the bytes to form the reversed 32-bit integer.
4. Return the result in **a0**.

The C code that calls the **reverse_bytes** procedure is shown in **Listing 26**.

Listing 26.

```
#include <stdio.h>

// Declare the assembly procedure
extern unsigned int reverse_bytes(unsigned int value);

int main() {
    unsigned int value = 0xAC9D37BF;
    unsigned int reversed = reverse_bytes(value);
    printf("Original: 0x%08X, Reversed: 0x%08X\n", value, reversed);
    return 0;
}
```

The application produces the following output:

Original: 0xAC9D37BF, Reversed: 0xBF379DAC

Bit operations

Using RV32 assembly for bit operations is highly effective, especially when performance and efficiency are critical. Assembly language provides direct access to hardware capabilities, minimal overhead, and precise control over the execution, making it ideal for low-level and performance-sensitive applications.

Example 1

Below is an example of an RV32 inline assembly procedure (**Listing 1**) that calculates the number of set bits (also known as the population count) in an integer and returns the result to C code.

Listing 1.

```
#include <stdio.h>

// Function to count the number of 1 bits in an integer
unsigned int count_one_bits(unsigned int n) {
    unsigned int count;
    asm volatile (
        "li t0, 0;"        // t0 = count = 0
        "li t1, 1;"        // t1 = mask = 1
    "loop:"
        "and t2, %1, t1;"  // t2 = n & mask
        "beqz t2, skip;"   // if (t2 == 0) skip
        "addi t0, t0, 1;"  // count++
    "skip:"
        "slli t1, t1, 1;"  // mask <<= 1
        "bnez t1, loop;"   // if (mask != 0) loop
        "mv %0, t0;"       // count = t0
        : "=r" (count)
        : "r" (n)
        : "t0", "t1", "t2"
    );
    return count;
}

int main() {
    unsigned int num = 51231779;  // Example number
    unsigned int result = count_one_bits(num);
    printf("Number of 1 bits in %u is %u\n", num, result);
    return 0;
}
```

Explanation

1. **Input and Output**: The function **count_one_bits** takes an unsigned integer n as input and returns the count of "1" bits.
2. **Assembly Code**:
   - **li t0, 0**: initializes the count to 0.
   - **li t1, 1**: initializes the mask to 1.
   - The **loop** label marks the start of the loop.
   - **and t2, %1, t1**: performs bitwise AND between the input number `n` and the current mask.
   - **beqz t2, skip**: branches to skip if the result of the AND operation is 0.
   - **addi t0, t0, 1**: increments the count if a "1" bit is found.
   - **skip**: is the label for skipping the increment.
   - **slli t1, t1, 1**: shifts the mask to the left.
   - **bnez t1, loop**: branches back to the loop if the mask is not zero.
   - **mv %0, t0**: moves the count to the output variable.
3. **Clobbers**: The registers **t0, t1**, and **t2** are listed as clobbered because they are used within the assembly block.
4. **Result**: The function returns the count of "1" bits to the calling C code.

Example 2

In this example, an RV32 inline assembly procedure (**Listing 2**) calculates the number of "0" bits in a 32-bit integer and returns the result to C code.

Listing 2.

```
#include <stdio.h>

// Function to count the number of 0 bits in an integer
unsigned int count_zero_bits(unsigned int n) {
    unsigned int count;
    asm volatile (
        "li t0, 0;"        // t0 = count = 0
        "li t1, 1;"        // t1 = mask = 1
        "li t3, 32;"       // t3 = bit count = 32
```

```
"loop:"
    "and t2, %1, t1;"      // t2 = n & mask
    "bnez t2, skip;"       // if (t2 != 0) skip
    "addi t0, t0, 1;"      // count++
"skip:"
    "slli t1, t1, 1;"      // mask <<= 1
    "addi t3, t3, -1;"     // bit count--
    "bnez t3, loop;"       // if (bit count != 0) loop
    "mv %0, t0;"           // count = t0
    : "=r" (count)
    : "r" (n)
    : "t0", "t1", "t2", "t3"
);
    return count;
}

int main() {
    unsigned int num = -51;  // Example number
    unsigned int result = count_zero_bits(num);
    printf("Number of 0 bits in %u is %u\n", num, result);
    return 0;
}
```

Explanation:

1. **Input and Output**: The function **count_zero_bits** takes an unsigned integer n as input and returns the count of "0" bits.

2. **Assembly Code**:
   - **li t0, 0**: initializes the count to 0.
   - **li t1, 1**: initializes the mask to 1.
   - **li t3, 32**: initializes the bit count to 32 (since we are working with 32-bit integers).
   - The **loop** label marks the start of the loop.
   - **and t2, %1, t1**: performs bitwise AND between the input number `n` and the current mask.
   - **bnez t2, skip**: branches to skip if the result of the AND operation is not zero.
   - **addi t0, t0, 1**: increments the count if a "0" bit is found.
   - **skip**: is the label for skipping the increment.
   - **slli t1, t1, 1**: shifts the mask to the left.

- **addi t3, t3, -1**: decrements the bit count.
- **bnez t3, loop**: branches back to the loop if the bit count is not zero.
- **mv %0, t0**: moves the count to the output variable.
3. **Clobbers**: The registers **t0, t1, t2,** and **t3** are listed as clobbered because they are used within the assembly block.
4. **Result**: The function returns the count of "0" bits to the calling C code.

Example 3

The code in this example allows to effectively set a specific bit in a **uint32** variable using RV32 assembly. The procedure is called from C code.
The procedure takes two parameters:
- The address of a 32-bit unsigned integer variable.
- The index of the bit to set (0-31).

The procedure sets the specified bit in the variable. Here's the RV32 assembly procedure to accomplish this (**Listing 3**):

Listing 3.

```
.section .text
.global set_bit

set_bit:
  # Arguments:
  #   a0: Address of the uint32 variable
  #   a1: Bit index

  # Load the value at the given address into register t0
    lw t0, 0(a0)

  # Calculate the mask for the bit
    addi t1, x0, 1   # Load 1 into t1
    sll t1, t1, a1      # Shift left by the bit index

  # Set the bit by ORing the mask with the value
    or t0, t0, t1
```

```
# Store the updated value back to memory
    sw t0, 0(a0)

# Return
    ret
```

Explanation

- **.global set_bit**: Makes the **set_bit** label globally visible, allowing it to be called from C code.
- **lw t0, 0(a0)**: Loads the 32-bit word at the address in register **a0** into register **t0**.
- **addi t1, x0, 1**: Loads the value 1 into register **t1**.
- **sll t1, t1, a1**: Shifts the value in **t1** left by the number of bits specified in **a1**. This creates a mask with the desired bit set.
- **or t0, t0, t1**: Performs a bitwise OR operation between the value in **t0** and the mask in **t1**, setting the specified bit in **t0**.
- **sw t0, 0(a0)**: Stores the updated value from **t0** back to the memory address in **a0**.
- **ret**: Returns from the function.

To call the **set_bit ()** function from C, we can use the following code (**Listing 4**):

Listing 4.

```
#include <stdint.h>
#include <stdio.h>

// Declaration of the assembly function
extern void set_bit(uint32_t *var, uint32_t bit);

int main() {
    uint32_t my_var = 0;
    uint32_t bit_to_set = 11; // For example, set the bit 11

    set_bit(&my_var, bit_to_set);

    // Now my_var should have the 11th bit set (i.e., my_var = 0x800)
```

```c
    printf("Updated Value = 0x%X\n", my_var);
    return 0;
}
```

Note:
The specific calling convention (argument passing, return value) might vary depending on the compiler and target platform. Ensure that the C calling convention matches the assembly procedure.

Example 4

The code in this example allows to effectively clear a specific bit in a **uint32** variable using RV32 assembly. The procedure is called from C code.
The procedure takes two parameters:
- The address of a 32-bit unsigned integer variable.
- The index of the bit to set (0-31).

The procedure clears the specified bit in the variable. Here's the RV32 assembly procedure to accomplish this (**Listing 5**):

Listing 5.

```
.section text
.global clear_bit

clear_bit:
  # Arguments:
  #   a0: Address of the uint32 variable
  #   a1: Bit index

  # Load the value at the given address into register t0
    lw t0, 0(a0)

  # Calculate the mask for the bit
    addi t1, x0, 1     # Load 1 into t1
    sll t1, t1, a1     # Shift left by the bit index

  # Invert the mask to clear the bit
```

```
    xori t1, t1, -1

# Clear the bit by ANDing the mask with the value
    and t0, t0, t1

# Store the updated value back to memory
    sw t0, 0(a0)

# Return
    ret
```

Explanation

The only significant change from the previous code (see **Example 3**) is the inversion of the mask.

- **xori t1, t1, -1**: This inverts the bits in **t1**, creating a mask with all bits set except the desired bit.
- **and t0, t0, t1**: Performs a bitwise AND operation, clearing the specified bit in **t0**.

The rest of the code remains the same, loading the value, storing the result, and returning.

To call the **clear_bit()** function from C, we can use the following code (**Listing 6**):

Listing 6.

```c
#include <stdint.h>
#include <stdio.h>

// Declaration of the assembly function
extern void clear_bit(uint32_t *var, uint32_t bit);

int main() {
    uint32_t my_var = 0xF;
    uint32_t bit_to_clear = 2; // For example, clear bit 2

    clear_bit(&my_var, bit_to_clear);

    // Now my_var should have the 2nd bit cleared (i.e., my_var = 0x0B)
    printf("Updated Value = 0x%X\n", my_var);
    return 0;
```

}

The C-side code would be similar to the previous example, but calling the **clear_bit** function instead.

Note:
As mentioned before, the specific calling convention might vary depending on the compiler and target platform. Ensure that the C calling convention matches the assembly procedure.

Example 5

The code in this example allows to effectively toggle a specific bit in a **uint32** variable using RV32 assembly. The procedure is called from C code.
The procedure takes two parameters:
- The address of a 32-bit unsigned integer variable.
- The index of the bit to set (0-31).

The procedure toggles the specified bit in the variable. Here's the RV32 assembly procedure to accomplish this (**Listing 7**):

Listing 7.

```
.section text
.global toggle_bit

toggle_bit:
  # Arguments:
  #   a0: Address of the uint32 variable
  #   a1: Bit index

  # Load the value at the given address into register t0
    lw t0, 0(a0)

  # Calculate the mask for the bit
    addi t1, x0, 1  # Load 1 into t1
    sll t1, t1, a1  # Shift left by the bit index

  # Toggle the bit by XORing the mask with the value
```

```
    xor t0, t0, t1

# Store the updated value back to memory
    sw t0, 0(a0)

# Return
    ret
```

Explanation

The key operation here is the XOR (exclusive OR) operation.

- **xor t0, t0, t1**: This toggles the specified bit in **t0**. If the bit is 0, it becomes 1; if it's 1, it becomes 0.

The rest of the code remains the same as before, loading the value, creating the mask, and storing the result.

The C-side code (**Listing 8**) would be similar to the previous examples, but calling the **toggle_bit** function instead. Also, in order to observe how the specified value changes after a bit has been toggled, a few **printf** functions were added.

Listing 8.

```c
#include <stdint.h>
#include <stdio.h>

// Declaration of the assembly function
extern void toggle_bit(uint32_t *var, uint32_t bit);

int main() {
    uint32_t my_var = 0x3;
    uint32_t bit_to_toggle = 1; // For example, toggle bit 1

    // Now my_var should have the 1st bit toggled 2 times
    printf("Initial Value = 0x%X\n", my_var);
    toggle_bit(&my_var, bit_to_toggle);
    printf("1.Toggled Value = 0x%X\n", my_var);
    toggle_bit(&my_var, bit_to_toggle);
    printf("2.Toggled value = 0x%X\n", my_var);
    return 0;
}
```

Example 6

Below is an example of an RV32 assembly procedure (**Listing 9**) that reverses the order of bits in a byte and returns the result to C code. This procedure uses a simple bitwise approach to reverse the bits.

Listing 9.

```
.section .text
.global reverse_bits
reverse_bits:
    addi sp, sp, -16      # Allocate stack space
    sw ra, 12(sp)         # Save return address
    sw a0, 8(sp)          # Save input byte

    li t0, 0         # Initialize result to 0
    li t1, 8         # Initialize bit counter to 8

  reverse_loop:
    slli t2, a0, 31       # Extract the leftmost bit of the input byte
    srli t2, t2, 31       # Move the bit to the least significant position
    slli t0, t0, 1        # Shift result left by 1 bit
    or t0, t0, t2         # OR the result with the extracted bit
    srli a0, a0, 1        # Shift input byte right by 1 bit
    addi t1, t1, -1       # Decrement bit counter
    bnez t1, reverse_loop # Repeat until all bits are processed

    mv a0, t0             # Move result to return register

    lw ra, 12(sp)         # Restore return address
    addi sp, sp, 16       # Deallocate stack space
    ret                   # Return to caller
```

Explanation

Assembly Code:

- **Prologue**: Allocate stack space and save the return address and input byte.
- **Initialization**: Set the result to 0 and initialize the bit counter to 8.
- **Loop**:
    - Extract the least significant bit (LSB) of the input byte and add it to the result.
    - Shift the result left by 1 bit and OR it with the extracted bit.
    - Shift the input byte right by 1 bit.
    - Decrement the bit counter and repeat until all bits are processed.

Epilogue: Restore the return address and deallocate stack space.

The C code to call the assembly procedure **reverse_bits** is shown in **Listing 10**.

Listing 10.

```
#include <stdio.h>

extern unsigned char reverse_bits(unsigned char byte);

int main() {
    unsigned char byte = 0x5D; // 01011101
    unsigned char reversed = reverse_bits(byte);
    printf("Original byte: 0x%02X\n", byte);
    printf("Reversed byte: 0x%02X\n", reversed);
    return 0;
}
```

Explanation of the C Code:
- Define the **reverse_bits** function as an external function.
- Call the function with a test byte and print the original and reversed bytes.

The application produces the following output:

Original byte: 0x5D
Reversed byte: 0xBA

Processing character strings

Processing character strings with RISC-V assembly involves several steps, including loading the string into memory, iterating through each character, and performing desired operations such as copying, comparing, or modifying characters. This section includes several examples that demonstrates how to use the RISC-V assembler to process character strings.

Example 1

Here's C code together with an RV32 inline assembly procedure (**Listing 1**) that reverses the order of bytes in a character string.

```c
#include <stdio.h>
#include <string.h>

// Declaration of the assembly function
void reverse_string(char *str, int len);

int main() {
    char str[] = "Hello, World!";
    int len = strlen(str);

    printf("Original string: %s\n", str);

    // Call the assembly function to reverse the string
    reverse_string(str, len);
    printf("Reversed string: %s\n", str);
    return 0;
}

void reverse_string(char *str, int len) {
    asm volatile (
        "add t0, %0, %1\n\t"   // t0 = str + len
        "addi t0, t0, -1\n\t"  // t0 points to last char
    "1:\n\t"
        "bge %0, t0, 2f\n\t"   // if str >= t0, exit loop
        "lb t1, 0(%0)\n\t"     // load byte from str
```

```
    "lb t2, 0(t0)\n\t"        // load byte from t0
    "sb t2, 0(%0)\n\t"        // store t2 to str
    "sb t1, 0(t0)\n\t"        // store t1 to t0
    "addi %0, %0, 1\n\t"      // increment str
    "addi t0, t0, -1\n\t"     // decrement t0
    "j 1b\n\t"                // jump to start of loop
  "2:\n\t"
    : "+r" (str)
    : "r" (len)
    : "t0", "t1", "t2"
  );
}
```

This C code does the following:
- It includes necessary header files.
- It declares the **reverse_string** function, which is implemented in assembly.
- In the main function, it:
  - Defines a sample string "Hello, World!"
  - Calculates the length of the string using **strlen**.
  - Prints the original string.
  - Calls the **reverse_string** function with the string and its length as arguments.
  - Prints the reversed string.

When compiled and run, this program would output:

Original string: Hello, World!
Reversed string: !dlroW ,olleH

Example 2

Here's an RV32 inline assembly procedure (**Listing 2**) that changes all characters in a string to uppercase, along with C code.

Listing 2.

```c
#include <stdio.h>
#include <string.h>

void to_uppercase(char *str, int len) {
    asm volatile (
    "1:\n\t"
        "beqz %1, 2f\n\t"      // if len == 0, exit loop
        "lb t0, 0(%0)\n\t"     // load byte from str
        "li t1, 'a'\n\t"       // load 'a' into t1
        "li t2, 'z'\n\t"       // load 'z' into t2
        "blt t0, t1, 3f\n\t"   // if char < 'a', skip
        "bgt t0, t2, 3f\n\t"   // if char > 'z', skip
        "addi t0, t0, -32\n\t" // convert to uppercase
        "sb t0, 0(%0)\n\t"     // store byte back to str
    "3:\n\t"
        "addi %0, %0, 1\n\t"   // increment str
        "addi %1, %1, -1\n\t"  // decrement len
        "j 1b\n\t"             // jump to start of loop
    "2:\n\t"
        : "+r" (str), "+r" (len)
        : "t0", "t1", "t2"
    );
}

int main() {
    char str[] = "Hello, World! 123";
    int len = strlen(str);

    printf("Original string: %s\n", str);

    // Call the assembly function to convert to uppercase
    to_uppercase(str, len);

    printf("Uppercase string: %s\n", str);

    return 0;
}
```

This code does the following:

1. The **to_uppercase** function uses inline assembly to convert the string to uppercase:
   - It loops through each character of the string.
   - For each character, it checks if it's between `a` and `z'`
   - If it is, it subtracts 32 from the ASCII value to convert it to uppercase.
   - The loop continues until all characters have been processed.

2. The **main** function:
   - Defines a sample string "Hello, World! 123"
   - Calculates the length of the string
   - Prints the original string
   - Calls the **to_uppercase** function
   - Prints the resulting uppercase string

When compiled and run, this program would output:

Original string: Hello, World! 123
Uppercase string: HELLO, WORLD! 123

Example 3

Below is the RV32 assembly procedure code (**Listing 3**) that replaces all dot (`.`) characters with spaces (` `). We assume that:
- The string is null-terminated.
- The string is passed as a pointer in the first argument register (a0).
- The procedure modifies the string in-place.
- The procedure is called from C code according to calling convention (for parameter passing and return value).

Listing 3.

```
.section text
.globl replace_dot_with_space

replace_dot_with_space:
  # Save registers used
    addi sp, sp, -16
    sw ra, 12(sp)
```

```
    sw s0, 8(sp)
    sw s1, 4(sp)
    sw s2, 0(sp)

# s0: pointer to the string
    mv s0, a0
loop:
    lb s1, 0(s0)      # Load a character
    beqz s1, end      # End of string if null character
    li s2, '.'          # Load '.' character for comparison
    bne s1, s2, next  # If not '.', go to next character
    li s1, ' '          # Replace with ' '
    sb s1, 0(s0)      # Store the replaced character
next:
    addi s0, s0, 1    # Increment pointer
    j loop
end:
# Restore registers
    lw s2, 0(sp)
    lw s1, 4(sp)
    lw s0, 8(sp)
    lw ra, 12(sp)
    addi sp, sp, 16
    ret
```

Explanation:
Function prologue:
- Saves registers **ra**, **s0**, **s1**, and **s2** on the stack.
- Moves the pointer to the string from **a0** to **s0**.

Loop:
- Loads a character from the current position into s1.
- Checks for the end of the string (null character).
- Compares the loaded character with `.`.
- If not `.`, jumps to the next character.
- Otherwise, replaces the character with ` ` and stores it back.
- Increments the pointer to the next character.
- Jumps back to the beginning of the loop.

Function epilogue:

- Restores saved registers.
- Returns from the function.

The C code that call the assembly procedure **replace_dot_with_space** is shown in **Listing 4**.

Listing 4.

```
#include <stdio.h>

void replace_dot_with_space(char *str);

int main() {
  char str[] = "This...is...a...test...!";
  replace_dot_with_space(str);
  printf("%s\n", str);
  return 0;
}
```

The application produces the following output:

This is a test !

Example 4

Below is an example (**Listing 5**) of an RV32 assembly procedure that compares two character strings and returns 0 if the strings are equal, otherwise returns 1. This procedure can be called from C code.

Listing 5.

```
#include <stdio.h>

int strcmp_asm(const char *s1, const char *s2) {
    int result;
    asm volatile(
        "li t0, 0\n"          // Initialize result to 0
        "mv a0, %1\n"         // Load address of s1 into a0
```

```
        "mv a1, %2\n"          // Load address of s2 into a1
    "loop:\n"
        "lb t1, (a0)\n"                // Load byte from s1\n"
        "lb t2, (a1)\n"                // Load byte from s2\n"
        "beqz t1, equal\n"         // If s1 is null, check if s2 is also null\n"
        "beqz t2, not_equal\n"    // If s2 is null, strings are not equal\n"
        "bne t1, t2, not_equal\n" // Compare bytes, branch if not equal\n"
        "addi a0, a0, 1\n"             // Increment s1 pointer\n"
        "addi a1, a1, 1\n"             // Increment s2 pointer\n"
        "j loop\n"                     // Continue loop\n"
    "equal:\n"
        "beqz  t2, equal_end\n"    // If s2 is also null, strings are equal\n"
        "j      not_equal\n"          //Otherwise, strings are not equal\n"
    "equal_end:\n"
        "li t0, 0\n"                   // Set result to 0 for equal strings\n"
        "j  end\n"
    "not_equal:\n"
        "li t0, 1\n"                   //Set result to 1 for not equal strings\n"
    "end:\n"
        "mv %0, t0\n"              // Move result to return register\n"
        : "=r" (result)
        : "r" (s1), "r" (s2)
        : "t0", "t1", "t2", "a0", "a1"
    );
    return result;
}

int main() {
    const char *str1 = "1234567890";
    const char *str2 = "1234567810";
    int result = strcmp_asm(str1, str2);
    printf("Result: %d\n", result);
    return 0;
}
```

Explanation:

- The **strcmp_asm** function takes two const char * arguments and returns an integer.
- The inline assembly block performs the string comparison.
- Registers **t0**, **t1**, and **t2** are used for temporary values.

- Registers **a0** and **a1** hold the addresses of the input strings.
- The **loop** label marks the beginning of the comparison loop.
- The **equal** and **not_equal** labels handle the cases where strings are equal or not equal.
- The **end** label marks the end of the assembly block.
- The **result** variable is used to store the return value.

Example 5

In this example, the RV32 assembly procedure (**Listing 6**) will count the occurrences of a specific character in a string.

Listing 6.

```
.section .text
.global CountChar

# Input:
#   - a0: Pointer to the string
#   - a1: Character to count
# Output:
#   - Returns the count in a0

CountChar:
    xor t0, t0, t0       # Initialize count (t0) to zero
    mv t1, a1            # Load the character to search for (a1)
Loop:
    lbu t2, 0(a0)           # Load a byte from the string
    beqz t2, EndOfP         # If null terminator (end of string), exit loop
    beq t2, t1, Increasing  # If character matches, increment count
    addi a0, a0, 1          # Move to the next character
    j Loop

Increasing:
    addi t0, t0, 1     # Increment count
    addi a0, a0, 1     # Move to the next character
    j Loop
```

```
EndOfP:
    mv a0, t0        # Return the count
    ret
```

The C code that calls this assembly procedure **CountChar** is shown below (**Listing 7**).

Listing 7.

```
#include <stdio.h>

extern int CountChar(const char* str, char ch);

int main() {
    const char* myString = "Hello, world! How many 'e' characters are here?";
    char searchChar = 'e';

    int count = CountChar(myString, searchChar);
    printf("Number of occurrences of '%c': %d\n", searchChar, count);

    return 0;
}
```

In this example, we assume that the input string is null-terminated. The **CountChar** function takes the pointer to the string and the character to count. It returns the count of occurrences.

The application provides the following output:

Number of occurrences of 'e': 6

Example 6

In this example, the assembly procedure (**Listing 8**) searches for a substring in a character string. If the substring is found, the procedure returns the index of the first element of the substring to the main C procedure. If the substring is not found, the procedure returns -1.
In this procedure, we use the following approach:

75

- Iterate through the main string character by character.
- For each character, compare the subsequent characters with the substring characters.
- If a mismatch occurs, move to the next character in the main string.
- If all characters match, return the index of the first character of the substring.
- If the end of the main string is reached without a match, return -1.

Listing 8.

```
# Arguments:
#   a0: Address of the main string
#   a1: Address of the substring
#   a2: Length of the substring
# Return value:
#   a0: Index of the first element of the substring, or -1 if not found

.section text
.globl find_substring

find_substring:
  # Prologue
    addi sp, sp, -16     # Allocate stack space for ra, s0, s1, s2
    sw ra, 12(sp)
    sw s0, 8(sp)
    sw s1, 4(sp)
    sw s2, 0(sp)

  # Initialize registers

    mv s0, a0    # Address of main string
    mv s1, a1    # Address of substring
    mv s2, a2    # Length of substring
    li a0, -1    # Default return value (not found)
    li t0, 0     # Index of current character in main string

  loop:
    lb t1, (s0)             # Load current character from main string
    beqz t1, not_found   # End of main string reached
```

```
# Check if the next 's2' characters match the substring
    mv t2, s0     # Save current position in main string
    mv t3, s1     # Save address of substring
    li t4, 0      # Index within substring

  inner_loop:
    lb t5, (t2)   # Load character from main string
    lb t6, (t3)   # Load character from substring
    bne t5, t6, outer_loop  # Characters don't match
    addi t2, t2, 1
    addi t3, t3, 1
    addi t4, t4, 1
    blt t4, s2, inner_loop  # Continue if not at end of substring

# Substring found!
    mv a0, t0  # Return index of first character
    j end

  outer_loop:
    addi s0, s0, 1   # Move to next character in main string
    addi t0, t0, 1   # Increment index
    j loop

  not_found:
# Substring not found

  end:
# Epilogue
    lw ra, 12(sp)
    lw s0, 8(sp)
    lw s1, 4(sp)
    lw s2, 0(sp)
    addi sp, sp, 16
    ret
```

Explanation

- The code starts by setting up the stack frame and initializing registers.
- The outer loop iterates through the main string.

- The inner loop compares the current substring with the corresponding characters in the main string.
- If a mismatch occurs, the outer loop continues.
- If the entire substring matches, the index is stored in **a0** and the function returns.
- If the end of the main string is reached without a match, -1 is returned.

Note:
- This code assumes that the strings are null-terminated.
- For efficiency, it would be worth considering specialized string instructions if available on specific RV32 architecture.
- Error handling for invalid input (e.g., null pointers) can be added.

The C Code that calls the assembly procedure **find_substring** is shown below (**Listing 9**).

Listing 9.

```
#include <stdio.h>
#include <string.h>

extern int find_substring(char *main_str, char *sub_str, int sub_len);

int main() {
    char main_str[] = "Hello, world!#1234567890.";
    char sub_str[] = "#1";

    int index = find_substring(main_str, sub_str, strlen(sub_str));

    if (index != -1) {
        printf("Substring found at index %d\n", index);
    } else {
        printf("Substring not found\n");
    }

    return 0;
}
```

Explanation:
- **Include header**: Includes the standard input/output library (stdio.h) for printing.
- **External declaration**: Declares the **find_substring** function as an external function (defined in assembly).
- **Main function**:
  - Defines the main string and substring.
  - Calls the **find_substring** function with the main string, substring, and substring length as arguments.
  - Prints the index if the substring is found, otherwise prints "Substring not found".

The application produces the following result:

Substring found at index 13

Example 7

In this example, the RV32 assembly procedure (**Listing 10**) searches for the matched elements in two character strings of the same length. The assembly procedure returns the number of the matched elements or 0 if no matched elements found.

Listing 10.

```
.section .text
.global count_matched_chars

count_matched_chars:
    # Function parameters:
    # a0: pointer to the first string
    # a1: pointer to the second string
    # a2: length of the strings

    add t0, zero, zero    # t0 will be used to count matches
    add t1, zero, zero    # t1 will be used as an index
```

```
count_matched_loop:
  beq t1, a2, count_matched_done # If index equals length, we are done
  lb t2, 0(a0)         # Load byte from first string
  lb t3, 0(a1)         # Load byte from second string
  beq t2, t3, count_increment   # If the characters match,
                                #increment the counter
  j count_continue

count_increment:
  addi t0, t0, 1       # Increment the match counter

count_continue:
  addi a0, a0, 1       # Move to the next character in the first string
  addi a1, a1, 1       # Move to the next character in the second string
  addi t1, t1, 1       # Increment the index
  j count_matched_loop

count_matched_done:
  mv a0, t0            # Move the match count to the return register
  ret                  # Return to the caller
```

Explanation
Function Declaration and Parameter Setup:
- The function is declared as **.global count_matched_chars**.
- The parameters are as follows:
- **a0**: Pointer to the first string.
- **a1**: Pointer to the second string.
- **a2**: Length of the strings.

Initialization:
- **t0** is initialized to 0 and will be used to count the matches.
- **t1** is initialized to 0 and will be used as an index to traverse the strings.

Loop:
- The loop starts with **count_matched_loop** and checks if **t1** equals **a2** (length of the strings). If they are equal, the loop ends.
- Inside the loop, characters from both strings are loaded into **t2** and **t3** respectively.

- If the characters match (**beq t2, t3**), the counter **t0** is incremented.
- The pointers **a0** and **a1** are incremented to point to the next characters in their respective strings.
- The index **t1** is incremented.
- The loop continues until all characters are compared.

Return:
- When the loop is done, the count of matched characters (**t0**) is moved to **a0** which is the return register.
- The function returns to the caller with **ret**.

Below (**Listing 11**) is the C code that calls the assembly function **count_matched_chars**.

Listing 11.

```
#include <stdio.h>

// Declaration of the assembly function
extern int count_matched_chars(char *str1, char *str2, int length);

int main() {
    char str1[] = "HELLo";
    char str2[] = "hxlxo";
    int length = 5;

    int matches = count_matched_chars(str1, str2, length);

    printf("Number of matched characters: %d\n", matches);
    return 0;
}
```

In this code, the **count_matched_chars** function is called with two strings and their length, and it returns the number of matched characters. The result is then printed.

The application produces the following output:

Number of matched characters: 1

Processing floating-point numbers

In the RV32 assembly language, floating-point operations are supported through the use of the RISC-V `S` and `D` extensions. These extensions add support for single-precision (32-bit) and double-precision (64-bit) floating-point arithmetic, respectively.

Here's a brief overview of how floating-point operations are supported:

1. **Floating-Point Register File**
   - **Floating-Point Registers**: The RISC-V architecture includes a set of floating-point registers separate from the integer registers. For single-precision, there are 32 floating-point registers (`f0` to `f31`), and for double-precision, there are also 32 registers (`f0` to `f31`).

2. **Floating-Point Instructions**
   - **Arithmetic Instructions**: The `S` and `D` extensions define a set of instructions for floating-point arithmetic operations such as addition, subtraction, multiplication, division, and square root. Examples include:
     - FADD.S (single-precision addition)
     - FSUB.S (single-precision subtraction)
     - FMUL.S (single-precision multiplication)
     - FDIV.S (single-precision division)
     - FSQRT.S (single-precision square root)
     - FADD.D (double-precision addition)
     - FSUB.D (double-precision subtraction)
     - FMUL.D (double-precision multiplication)
     - FDIV.D (double-precision division)
     - FSQRT.D (double-precision square root)

   - **Conversion Instructions**: There are instructions to convert between floating-point and integer representations, such as:
     - FTOI.S (convert from single-precision floating-point to integer)

♦ ITOF.S (convert from integer to single-precision floating-point)

- **Comparison Instructions**: Floating-point comparisons can be performed using instructions like:
  ♦ FEQ.S (floating-point equal, single-precision)
  ♦ FLT.S (floating-point less-than, single-precision)
  ♦ FLE.S (floating-point less-than-or-equal, single-precision)

3. **Special Floating-Point Control and Status**
   - **Control and Status Registers**: The floating-point unit (FPU) has control and status registers to handle exceptions and control rounding modes. These include:
     ♦ FCSR (Floating-Point Control and Status Register): Manages exceptions, rounding modes, and other floating-point status information.

4. **Usage**
   - Floating-point instructions operate on the floating-point registers and adhere to IEEE 754 standard formats for single and double precision.
   - The `S` and `D` extensions are optional, so they might not be implemented in all RISC-V processors. To utilize these features, the processor must support these extensions, and the programmer should ensure that the floating-point operations are enabled and correctly configured.

In summary, RV32 assembly language supports floating-point operations through a well-defined set of instructions and registers introduced by the `S` and `D` extensions. These extensions allow for a range of arithmetic, comparison, and conversion operations, enabling sophisticated numerical computations on RISC-V architectures.

Example 1

In this example, we use an RV32 assembly procedure (**Listing 1**) for conversion of two integers into a single-precision floating-point format and then divide the first floating-point number by the second one.

Before we dive into the code, let's clarify the requirements:

- **The RV32 assembly procedure**: Will take two integer parameters, convert them to single-precision floating-point numbers, divide one by the other, and return the floating-point result.
- **C code**: Will call the assembly procedure with two integer arguments and print the returned floating-point result.

We also assume that:

- We're using the standard RISC-V calling convention.
- The system has a floating-point unit (FPU) available.
- We're using single-precision floating-point numbers (float).

Listing 1.

```
.section .text
.global div_int_as_float

div_int_as_float:
  # Save registers used
    addi sp, sp, -16
    sw ra, 12(sp)
    sw a0, 8(sp)
    sw a1, 4(sp)

  # Convert integers to floats
    fcvt.s.w f0, a0
    fcvt.s.w f1, a1

  # Divide f0 by f1
    fdiv.s f0, f0, f1

  # Restore registers and return
    lw ra, 12(sp)
    lw a0, 8(sp)
    lw a1, 4(sp)
    addi sp, sp, 16
    fmv.x.w a0, f0
```

```
ret
```

Explanation

- **Save registers**: We save the return address (**ra**), **a0**, and **a1** on the stack to preserve their values.
- **Convert to float**: We convert the integer arguments in **a0** and **a1** to single-precision floating-point numbers and store them in **f0** and **f1**.
- **Divide**: We divide **f0** by **f1** and store the result in **f0**.
- **Restore registers**: We restore the saved registers from the stack.
- **Return**: We move the floating-point result in **f0** to the integer register **a0** (for return) and return from the function.

The C code is shown in **Listing 2**.

Listing 2.

```c
#include <stdio.h>

extern float div_int_as_float(int a, int b);

int main() {
  int x = -101, y = 29;
  float result = div_int_as_float(x, y);
  printf("Result: %f\n", result);
  return 0;
}
```

Explanation:

- **Include header**: Includes the standard input/output library.
- **External declaration**: Declares the assembly function **div_int_as_float** as an external function.
- **Main function**: Defines the **main** function.
- **Integer variables**: Declares integer variables **x** and **y**.
- **Function call**: Calls the assembly function with **x** and **y** as arguments and stores the result in result.
- **Print result**: Prints the calculated result.

Note:

- This code assumes a basic RISC-V architecture with an FPU. Specific implementations might require adjustments.
- For more complex floating-point operations or higher precision, we might need to use double-precision floating-point numbers and corresponding instructions.
- Error handling for division by zero is not implemented in this example.

The application produces the following output:

Result: -3.482759

Example 2

In this example, the RV32 assembly procedure **(Listing 3)** calculates the sum of two single-precision numbers and returns the result to the C procedure.

Listing 3.

```
.section .text        # Start of the code section
.global sum2floats    # Make the sum2floats function globally visible
sum2floats:           # Function label
    addi sp, sp, -16  # Allocate 16 bytes on the stack (adjust the stack
                      #pointer)
    sw a0, 12(sp)     # Store the first argument (a0) at offset 12 from the
                      # stack pointer
    sw a1, 8(sp)      # Store the second argument (a1) at offset 8 from
                      # the stack pointer
    flw fa4, 12(sp)   # Load the first argument (stored at 12(sp)) into
                      #floating-point register fa4
    flw fa5, 8(sp)    # Load the second argument (stored at 8(sp)) into
                      #floating-point register fa5
    fadd.s fa5, fa4, fa5  # Add the two floating-point numbers in fa4 and
                      #fa5, store the result in fa5
    fmv.x.w a0, fa5   # Move the result from floating-point register fa5 to
                      #integer register a0
    addi sp, sp, 16   # Deallocate the 16 bytes from the stack (restore the
                      #stack pointer)
```

```
ret                    # Return from the function
```

Detailed Explanation:
1. **Stack Allocation and Argument Storage**:
    - **addi sp, sp, -16**: Decrease the stack pointer by 16 bytes to allocate space on the stack.
    - **sw a0, 12(sp)**: Store the first floating-point argument (passed in **a0**) at offset 12 from the current stack pointer.
    - **sw a1, 8(sp)**: Store the second floating-point argument (passed in **a1**) at offset 8 from the current stack pointer.
2. **Loading Arguments into Floating-Point Registers**:
    - **flw fa4, 12(sp)**: Load the first floating-point argument from memory (12 bytes offset from the stack pointer) into the floating-point register **fa4**.
    - **flw fa5, 8(sp)**: Load the second floating-point argument from memory (8 bytes offset from the stack pointer) into the floating-point register **fa5**.
3. **Floating-Point Addition**:
    - **fadd.s fa5, fa4, fa5**: Add the values in **fa4** and **fa5**, storing the result back into **fa5**.
4. **Moving Result to Return Register**:
    - **fmv.x.w a0, fa5**: Move the result from the floating-point register **fa5** to the integer register **a0** (which is used for returning values).
5. **Stack Deallocation and Return**:
    - **addi sp, sp, 16**: Restore the stack pointer by adding back the 16 bytes previously allocated.
    - **ret**: Return from the function, with the result of the addition in a0.

Summary

The **sum2floats** function takes two single-precision floating-point numbers as input, adds them, and returns the result. The arguments are initially passed in integer registers **a0** and **a1**, stored on the stack, loaded into floating-point registers, added together, and the result is moved back to an integer register for returning. The stack is managed to preserve the original values and maintain proper function call conventions.

The C code that calls the function **sum2floats** is shown in **Listing 4**.

Listing 4.

```c
#include <stdio.h>

// Declare the assembly function prototype
extern float sum2floats(float a1, float a2);

int main() {
    float a1 = 3.33;
    float a2 = -5.83;
    float sum;

    // Call the assembly function
    sum = sum2floats(a1, a2);

    printf("Sum of elements: %f\n", sum);

    return 0;
}
```

Example 3

In this example, the RV32 assembly procedure (**Listing 5**) calculates the sum of 5 single-precision floating-point numbers. The procedure works as follows:

- Accepts a single parameter that is the pointer to an array of 5 single-precision floating-point numbers.
- Initializes a loop to iterate through each element of the array.
- Accumulates the sum of the elements in a floating-point register.
- Returns the sum.

Listing 5.

```
.section .text
.global sum5floats
sum5floats:
```

```
addi sp, sp, -16        # Allocate stack space
sw ra, 12(sp)           # Save return address
sw a0, 8(sp)            # Save the pointer to the array

# Initialize sum to 0.0
fmv.s.x fa0, zero

li t0, 5                # Loop counter (5 elements)
la t1, 0                # Array index offset

loop:
beqz t0, end            # If counter is zero, exit loop

# Load array element
lw t2, 8(sp)            # Load base address of array
add t3, t2, t1          # Calculate address of current element
flw fa1, 0(t3)          # Load current float element

# Add current element to sum
fadd.s fa0, fa0, fa1
addi t1, t1, 4          # Move to the next float element (4 bytes per float)
addi t0, t0, -1         # Decrement loop counter
j loop                  # Repeat the loop
end:
# Move the result to a0
fmv.x.w a0, fa0
lw ra, 12(sp)           # Restore return address
addi sp, sp, 16         # Restore stack pointer
ret                     # Return to caller
```

Explanation

1.Prologue: Adjust Stack Pointer:

```
addi sp, sp, -16
sw ra, 12(sp)
sw a0, 8(sp)
```

Allocate stack space and save the return address and the pointer to the array on the stack.

2.Initialize the Sum to 0:

```
fmv.s.x fa0, zero
```

Initialize the floating-point register **fa0** to 0.0, which will hold the accumulated sum.

3.Set Up the Loop Counter and Index:

```
li t0, 10
la t1, 0
```

4.Set the loop counter (t0) to 5 and initialize the index offset (t1) to 0. Loop to Accumulate the Sum

```
loop:
    beqz t0, end
    lw t2, 8(sp)
    add t3, t2, t1
    flw fa1, 0(t3)
    fadd.s fa0, fa0, fa1
    addi t1, t1, 4
    addi t0, t0, -1
    j loop
```

5.After the loop, move the sum from fa0 to a0, restore the return address and stack pointer, and return to the caller:

```
end:
    fmv.x.w a0, fa0
    lw ra, 12(sp)
    addi sp, sp, 16
    ret
```

Below (**Listing 6**) is the C code that calls the **sum5floats** assembly procedure. The code includes a declaration for the assembly procedure, an array of 5 single-precision floating-point numbers, and a call to the assembly procedure to calculate their sum.

Listing 6.

```c
#include <stdio.h>

// Declaration of the assembly procedure
extern float sum5floats(float* array);

int main() {
    // Initialize an array of 5 floating-point numbers
    float numbers[5] = {0.1, -75.26, 10.83, -90.4, 0.5};

    // Call the assembly procedure and store the result
    float result = sum5floats(numbers);

    // Print the result
    printf("Sum of the array elements: %f\n", result);

    return 0;
}
```

Notes
Ensure the assembly procedure **sum5floats** is properly linked with the C code during the compilation process. We might need to adjust the build commands to include both the C and assembly source files, depending on your build environment and toolchain.

The application produces the following output:

Sum of the array elements: -154.230011

Example 4

Below (**Listing 7**) is the RV32 assembly procedure that finds the maximum element in a 5-element single-precision floating-point array.

Listing 7.

```asm
.section .text
.global max5floats
```

```
max5floats:
    addi sp, sp, -16        # Allocate stack space
    sw ra, 12(sp)           # Save return address
    sw a0, 8(sp)            # Save the pointer to the array

  # Load the first element as the initial maximum
    lw t1, 8(sp)            # Load base address of array
    flw fa0, 0(t1)          # Load the first float element into fa0 (max)

    li t0, 4                # Loop counter (4 more elements to check)
    addi t1, t1, 4          # Point to the next element

loop:
    beqz t0, end            # If counter is zero, exit loop
    flw fa1, 0(t1)          # Load current float element
    fmax.s fa0, fa0, fa1    # Update fa0 to be the max of fa0 and fa1
    addi t1, t1, 4          # Move to the next float element (4 bytes per float)
    addi t0, t0, -1         # Decrement loop counter

    j loop                  # Repeat the loop
end:
  # Move the result to a0
    fmv.x.w a0, fa0

    lw ra, 12(sp)           # Restore return address
    addi sp, sp, 16         # Restore stack pointer
    ret                     # Return to caller
```

Explanation

1.Prologue: Adjust Stack Pointer

```
addi sp, sp, -16
sw ra, 12(sp)
sw a0, 8(sp)
```

Allocate stack space and save the return address and the pointer to the array on the stack.

2.Initialize Maximum with the First Element:

```
lw t1, 8(sp)
flw fa0, 0(t1)
```

Load the base address of the array and load the first float element into **fa0**, which is initially considered the maximum value.

3.Set Up the Loop Counter and Point to the Next Element:

```
li t0, 4
addi t1, t1, 4
```

Set the loop counter (t0) to 4 (since we have already loaded the first element) and update the pointer to the next element.
Loop to Find the Maximum Element:

```
loop:
   beqz t0, end
   flw fa1, 0(t1) fmax.s fa0, fa0, fa1
   addi t1, t1, 4 addi t0, t0, -1
   j loop
```

In the loop, check if the loop counter is zero (`beqz t0, end`). If not, load the current float element into **fa1**, update **fa0** to be the maximum of **fa0** and **fa1**, and then update the pointer and counter for the next iteration.

4.Epilogue: Move Result to `a0`, Restore Stack, and Return

```
end:
   fmv.x.w a0, fa0
   lw ra, 12(sp)
   addi sp, sp, 16
   ret
```

After the loop exits, move the maximum value from **fa0** to **a0**, restore the return address and stack pointer, and return to the caller.

Here (**Listing 8**) is the corresponding C code to call the **max5floats** assembly procedure.

Listing 8.

```c
#include <stdio.h>

// Declaration of the assembly procedure
extern float max5floats(float* array);

int main() {
    // Initialize an array of 5 floating-point numbers
    float numbers[5] = {-11.09, -3.3, -12.71, -5.92, -4.73};

    // Call the assembly procedure and store the result
    float max_value = max5floats(numbers);

    // Print the result
    printf("Maximum element in the array: %f\n", max_value);

    return 0;
}
```

The application produces the following output:

Maximum element in the array: -3.300000

Example 5

In this example, the assembly procedure (**Listing 9**) and C code (**Listing 10**) find the minimum element in a 5-element single-precision floating point array.

Listing 9.

```
.section .text
.global min5floats
min5floats:
    addi sp, sp, -16        # Allocate stack space
    sw ra, 12(sp)           # Save return address
    sw a0, 8(sp)            # Save the pointer to the array
```

```
# Load the first element as the initial maximum
    lw t1, 8(sp)          # Load base address of array
    flw fa0, 0(t1)        # Load the first float element into fa0 (max)

    li t0, 4              # Loop counter (4 more elements to check)
    addi t1, t1, 4        # Point to the next element
loop:
    beqz t0, end          # If counter is zero, exit loop
    flw fa1, 0(t1)        # Load current float element
    fmin.s fa0, fa0, fa1  # Update fa0 to be the max of fa0 and fa1
    addi t1, t1, 4        # Move to the next float element (4 bytes per float)
    addi t0, t0, -1       # Decrement loop counter
    j loop                # Repeat the loop

end:
    # Move the result to a0
    fmv.x.w a0, fa0
    lw ra, 12(sp)         # Restore return address
    addi sp, sp, 16       # Restore stack pointer
    ret                   # Return to caller
```

Listing 10.

```
#include <stdio.h>

// Declaration of the assembly procedure
extern float min5floats(float* array);

int main() {
    // Initialize an array of 5 floating-point numbers
    float numbers[5] = {1.1, -3.77, -2.12, 5.5, -4.94};

    // Call the assembly procedure and store the result
    float min_value = min5floats(numbers);

    // Print the result
    printf("Minimum element in the array: %f\n", min_value);

    return 0;
```

}

The application produces the following output:

Minimum element in the array: -4.940000

Example 6

In this example (**Listing 11**), the RV32 assembly procedure converts each element of a 5-element single-precision floating-point array into the corresponding absolute value.

Listing 11.

```
.section .text
.global abs5floats
abs5floats:
        addi sp, sp, -16        # Allocate stack space
        sw ra, 12(sp)           # Save return address
        sw a0, 8(sp)            # Save the pointer to the array

        li t0, 5                # Loop counter (5 elements)
        lw t1, 8(sp)            # Load base address of the array
    loop:
        beqz t0, end            # If counter is zero, exit loop
        flw fa0, 0(t1)          # Load current float element into fa0
        fabs.s fa0, fa0         # Compute absolute value of fa0
        fsw fa0, 0(t1)          # Store the absolute value back to the array
        addi t1, t1, 4          # Move to the next float element (4 bytes per float)
        addi t0, t0, -1         # Decrement loop counter
        j loop                  # Repeat the loop

end:
    lw ra, 12(sp)              # Restore return address
    addi sp, sp, 16            # Restore stack pointer
    ret                        # Return to caller
```

The corresponding C code to call the **abs5floats** assembly procedure is shown in **Listing 12**.

Listing 12.

```c
#include <stdio.h>

// Declaration of the assembly procedure
extern void abs5floats(float* array);

int main() {
    // Initialize an array of 5 floating-point numbers
    float numbers[5] = {-21.79, -43.38, -0.92, 15.5, 4.4};

    // Call the assembly procedure to compute absolute values
    abs5floats(numbers);

    // Print the result
    printf("Array with absolute values:\n");
    for (int i = 0; i < 5; i++) {
        printf("%f ", numbers[i]);
    }
    printf("\n");

    return 0;
}
```

The **main()** procedure calls the **abs5floats** assembly procedure, passing the array of floating-point numbers. The procedure will modify the array in place to contain the absolute values.

The application produces the following output:

Array with absolute values:
21.790001 43.380001 0.920000 15.500000 4.400000

Example 7

In this example, the assembly procedure (**Listing 13**) searches for the first negative element in a 5-element single-precision floating-point array and return the number of this element (if found) or -1 if nothing found.

Listing 13.

```
.section .text
.global find_first_negative
find_first_negative:
    addi sp, sp, -16        # Allocate stack space
    sw ra, 12(sp)           # Save return address
    sw a0, 8(sp)            # Save the pointer to the array
    li t0, 5                # Loop counter (5 elements)
    lw t1, 8(sp)            # Load base address of the array
    li t2, 0                # Initialize index counter
    fmv.s.x fa1, zero       # Load 0.0 into fa1 for comparison
loop:
    beqz t0, end            # If counter is zero, exit loop
    flw fa0, 0(t1)          # Load current float element into fa0
    flt.s t3, fa0, fa1      # Check if fa0 < 0.0
    bnez t3, found          # If fa0 is negative, jump to found
    addi t1, t1, 4          # Move to the next float element (4 bytes per float)
    addi t2, t2, 1          # Increment index counter
    addi t0, t0, -1         # Decrement loop counter
    j loop                  # Repeat the loop
end:
    li a0, -1               # No negative element found, return -1
    j exit
found:
    mv a0, t2               # If a negative element is found, move index to a0
exit:
    lw ra, 12(sp)           # Restore return address
    addi sp, sp, 16         # Restore stack pointer
    ret                     # Return to caller
```

Explanation

1.Prologue: Adjust Stack Pointer:
```
addi sp, sp, -16
sw ra, 12(sp)
sw a0, 8(sp)
```

Allocate stack space and save the return address and the pointer to the array on the stack.

2.Set Up the Loop Counter and Base Address:

```
li t0, 5
lw t1, 8(sp)
li t2, 0
fmv.s.x fa1, zero
li t0, 5
lw t1, 8(sp)
li t2, 0
fmv.s.x fa1, zero
```

Set the loop counter (**t0**) to 5 (since we have 5 elements), load the base address of the array into **t1**, initialize the index counter (**t2**) to 0, and load 0.0 into **fa1** for comparison.

3.Loop to Find the First Negative Element:

```
loop:
    beqz t0, end
    flw fa0, 0(t1)
    flt.s t3, fa0, fa1
    bnez t3, found
    addi t1, t1, 4
    addi t2, t2, 1
    addi t0, t0, -1
    j loop
```

In the loop, check if the loop counter is zero (`beqz t0, end`). If not, load the current float element into **fa0**, use `flt.s` to compare if **fa0** is less than **fa1** (0.0). If **fa0** is negative, **t3** will be non-zero and the procedure jumps to `found`. If not, update the pointer and counter for the next iteration.

4.End of Loop: Return -1 if No Negative Element Found:

```
end:
    li a0, -1
    j exit
```

found:
    mv a0, t2
exit:
    lw ra, 12(sp)
    addi sp, sp, 16
    ret

If the loop completes without finding a negative element, load -1 into **a0**. If a negative element is found, move the current index to **a0**. Then, restore the return address and stack pointer, and return to the caller.

The C code that calls the assembly procedure is shown in **Listing 14**.

Listing 14.

```
#include <stdio.h>

// Declaration of the assembly procedure
extern int find_first_negative(float* array);

int main() {
    // Initialize an array of 5 floating-point numbers
    float numbers[5] = {1.1, 3.3, 2.2, 5.5, -4.4};

    // Call the assembly procedure and store the result
    int index = find_first_negative(numbers);

    // Print the result
    if (index == -1) {
        printf("No negative element found in the array.\n");
    } else {
        printf("First negative element found at index: %d\n", index);
    }

    return 0;
}
```

The C code calls the **find_first_negative** assembly procedure, passing the array of floating-point numbers, and store the result in index. The application prints the index of the first negative element if found; otherwise, print a message indicating no negative element was found.

The application produces the following output:

First negative element found at index: 4

Example 8

In this example, the RV32 assembly procedure (**Listing 15**) calculates the number of negative elements in a 5-element single-precision floating-point array.

Listing 15.

```
.section .text
.global count_negative_elements
count_negative_elements:
    addi sp, sp, -16       # Allocate stack space
    sw ra, 12(sp)          # Save return address
    sw a0, 8(sp)           # Save the pointer to the array
    li t0, 5               # Loop counter (5 elements)
    lw t1, 8(sp)           # Load base address of the array

    li t2, 0               # Initialize element index counter
    li t4, 0               # Initialize negative element count to 0
    fmv.s.x fa1, zero      # Load 0.0 into fa1 for comparison
loop:
    beqz t0, end           # If counter is zero, exit loop
    flw fa0, 0(t1)         # Load current float element into fa0
    flt.s t3, fa0, fa1     # Check if fa0 < 0.0
    beqz t3, not_negative    # If fa0 is not negative, skip increment
    addi t4, t4, 1         # Increment negative element count
not_negative:
    addi t1, t1, 4         # Move to the next float element (4 bytes per float)
    addi t2, t2, 1         # Increment index counter
    addi t0, t0, -1        # Decrement loop counter
    j loop                 # Repeat the loop
end:
```

```
    mv a0, t4            # Move negative element count to a0
  exit:
    lw ra, 12(sp)        # Restore return address
    addi sp, sp, 16      # Restore stack pointer
    ret                  # Return to caller
```

Explanation

Prologue: Adjust Stack Pointer:

```
    addi sp, sp, -16
    sw ra, 12(sp)
    sw a0, 8(sp)
```

Allocate stack space and save the return address and the pointer to the array on the stack.

Set Up the Loop Counter, Base Address, and Initialize Counters:

```
    li t0, 5
    lw t1, 8(sp)
    li t2, 0
    li t4, 0
    fmv.s.x fa1, zero
```

Set the loop counter (**t0**) to 5 (since we have 5 elements), load the base address of the array into **t1**, initialize the index counter (**t2**) to 0, initialize the negative element count (**t4**) to 0, and load 0.0 into **fa1** for comparison.

Loop to Count Negative Elements:

```
  loop:
    beqz t0, end
    flw fa0, 0(t1)
    flt.s t3, fa0, fa1
    beqz t3, not_negative
    addi t4, t4, 1
  not_negative:
    addi t1, t1, 4
    addi t2, t2, 1
```

```
addi t0, t0, -1
j loop
```

In the loop, check if the loop counter is zero (`beqz t0, end`). If not, load the current float element into **fa0**, use `flt.s` to compare if **fa0** is less than **fa1** (0.0). If **fa0** is negative (**t3** is non-zero), increment the negative element count (**t4**). Regardless, move to the next element and update the index and loop counters.

End of Loop: Return Negative Element Count:

```
end:
  mv a0, t4
exit:
  lw ra, 12(sp)
  addi sp, sp, 16
  ret
```

After the loop completes, move the negative element count from **t4** to **a0**. Then, restore the return address and stack pointer, and return to the caller.

The C code for calling the assembly procedure is shown in **Listing 16**:

Listing 16.

```c
#include <stdio.h>

// Declaration of the assembly procedure
extern int count_negative_elements(float* array);

int main() {
    // Initialize an array of 5 floating-point numbers
    float numbers[5] = {34.16, 73.12, -82.55, 17.11, -74.9};

    // Call the assembly procedure and store the result
    int count = count_negative_elements(numbers);

    // Print the result
    printf("Number of negative elements in the array: %d\n", count);
```

        return 0;
}

The application produces the following output:

Number of negative elements in the array: 2

Example 9

The RV32 assembly procedure shown in **Listing 17** calculates the square root of each element in a 5-element array, and skips negative numbers. Here, we use the **fsqrt.s** instruction for the square root operation. We also need to check if the element is negative and skip it if so.

Listing 17.

```
.section .text
.global calculate_square_roots
calculate_square_roots:
        addi sp, sp, -16        # Allocate stack space
        sw ra, 12(sp)           # Save return address
        sw a0, 8(sp)            # Save the pointer to the array
        li t0, 5                # Loop counter (5 elements)
        lw t1, 8(sp)            # Load base address of the array
        fmv.s.x fa1, zero       # Load 0.0 into fa1 for comparison
    loop:
        beqz t0, end            # If counter is zero, exit loop
        flw fa0, 0(t1)          # Load current float element into fa0
        flt.s t3, fa0, fa1      # Check if fa0 < 0.0
        bnez t3, skip           # If fa0 is negative, skip to the next element
        fsqrt.s fa0, fa0        # Calculate the square root of fa0
        fsw fa0, 0(t1)          # Store the result back into the array
    skip:
        addi t1, t1, 4          # Move to the next float element (4 bytes per float)
        addi t0, t0, -1         # Decrement loop counter
        j loop                  # Repeat the loop
    end:
        lw ra, 12(sp)           # Restore return address
        addi sp, sp, 16         # Restore stack pointer
```

```
    ret                # Return to caller
```

Explanation

Prologue: Adjust Stack Pointer:

```
addi sp, sp, -16
sw ra, 12(sp)
sw a0, 8(sp)
```

Allocate stack space and save the return address and the pointer to the array on the stack.

Set Up the Loop Counter and Base Address:

```
li t0, 5
lw t1, 8(sp)
fmv.s.x fa1, zero
```

Set the loop counter (**t0**) to 5 (since we have 5 elements), load the base address of the array into **t1**, and load 0.0 into **fa1** for comparison.

Loop to Calculate Square Roots:

```
loop:
  beqz t0, end
  flw fa0, 0(t1)
  flt.s t3, fa0, fa1
  bnez t3, skip
  fsqrt.s fa0, fa0
  fsw fa0, 0(t1)
skip:
  addi t1, t1, 4
  addi t0, t0, -1
  j loop
```

In the loop, check if the loop counter is zero (`beqz t0, end`). If not, load the current float element into **fa0**, use `flt.s` to compare if **fa0** is less than **fa1** (0.0). If **fa0** is negative (**t3** is non-zero), skip the square root calculation and move to the next element. Otherwise, calculate the square root of **fa0** and store the result back into the array. Update the pointer and counter for the next iteration.

End of Loop:

```
end:
    lw ra, 12(sp)
    addi sp, sp, 16
    ret
```

This code fragment restores the return address and stack pointer, and return to the caller

Here's the C code to call the assembly procedure (**Listing 18**).

Listing 18.

```c
#include <stdio.h>

// Declaration of the assembly procedure
extern void calculate_square_roots(float* array);

int main() {
    // Initialize an array of 5 floating-point numbers
    float numbers[5] = {1.1, -3.3, 2.2, -5.5, 4.4};

    // Call the assembly procedure
    calculate_square_roots(numbers);

    // Print the result
    printf("Array after calculating square roots:\n");
    for (int i = 0; i < 5; i++) {
        printf("%f ", numbers[i]);
    }
    printf("\n");

    return 0;
}
```

The application produces the following output:

Array after calculating square roots:
1.048809 -3.300000 1.483240 -5.500000 2.097618

Example 10

In this example, the RV32 assembly procedure (**Listing 19**) compares two 5-element single-precision floating-point arrays and returns the number of mismatched elements.

Listing 19.

```
.section .text
.global count_mismatches
count_mismatches:
    addi sp, sp, -16
    sw ra, 12(sp)
    sw a0, 8(sp)
    sw a1, 4(sp)
    li t0, 5
    lw t1, 8(sp)
    lw t2, 4(sp)
    li t3, 0
  loop:
    beqz t0, end
    flw fa0, 0(t1)
    flw fa1, 0(t2)
    feq.s t4, fa0, fa1
    beqz t4, mismatch
  next:
    addi t1, t1, 4
    addi t2, t2, 4
    addi t0, t0, -1
    j loop
  mismatch:
    addi t3, t3, 1
    j next
  end:
    mv a0, t3
  exit:
```

```
lw ra, 12(sp)
addi sp, sp, 16
ret
```

Code Breakdown

1. **Prologue:**

   ```
   addi sp, sp, -16    # Adjust stack pointer
                       # to make room for saved registers
                       # (16 bytes).
   sw ra, 12(sp)       # Save return address (ra) to the stack.
   sw a0, 8(sp)        # Save first array pointer (a0) to the stack.
   sw a1, 4(sp)        # Save second array pointer (a1) to the stack.
   ```

   This part sets up the stack frame and saves the necessary registers.

2. **Initialization:**

   ```
   li t0, 5            # Load immediate value 5 into t0 (loop counter
                       # for 5 elements).
   lw t1, 8(sp)        # Load first array pointer (a0)
                       # from the stack into t1.
   lw t2, 4(sp)        # Load second array pointer (a1
                       # from the stack into t2.
   li t3, 0            # Initialize mismatch counter (t3) to 0.
   ```

   Initializes the loop counter to 5 and sets up pointers to the two arrays. **t3** will count the mismatched elements.

3. **Loop:**

   ```
   loop:
       beqz t0, end        # If t0 is 0, jump to the end (loop exit condition).
       flw fa0, 0(t1)      # Load the next element from the
                           # first array into fa0.
       flw fa1, 0(t2)      # Load the next element from the second array
                           # into fa1.
       feq.s t4, fa0, fa1  # Compare the two elements.
                           # If equal, set t4 to 1, otherwise 0.
       beqz t4, mismatch   # If the elements are not equal (t4 == 0),
                           # jump to mismatch.
   ```

This loop iterates over each element of the arrays. If the elements at the current position in the arrays are equal, the loop continues to the next iteration. If they are not equal, the code jumps to the `mismatch` label.

4. **Next Iteration**:
   next:

```
addi t1, t1, 4   # Increment the first array pointer (t1)
                 #to the next element.
addi t2, t2, 4   # Increment the second array pointer (t2) to the
                 # next element.
addi t0, t0, -1  # Decrement the loop counter (t0).
j loop           # Jump back to the start of the loop.
```

   Updates pointers to move to the next elements and decrements the loop counter. The loop then repeats.

5. **Mismatch Handling**:
   mismatch:

```
addi t3, t3, 1   # Increment the mismatch counter (t3).
j next           # Jump back to the next iteration.
```

   If a mismatch is detected, the mismatch counter **t3** is incremented.

6. **End of Loop**:
   end:

```
mv a0, t3        # Move the mismatch count
                 # into the return register (a0).
exit:
lw ra, 12(sp)    # Restore the return address (ra)
                 # from the stack.
addi sp, sp, 16  # Restore the stack pointer.
ret              # Return to the caller.
```

   Once the loop finishes, the mismatch counter **t3** is moved into **a0** to be returned to the caller. The stack is then restored, and the procedure returns.

Below is the C code to call the assembly procedure (**Listing 20**):

Listing 20.

```
#include <stdio.h>

// Declaration of the assembly procedure
extern int count_mismatches(float* array1, float* array2);

int main() {
    // Initialize two arrays of 5 floating-point numbers
    float array1[5] = {1.2, 2.2, 3.31, 4.4, 5.5};
    float array2[5] = {1.1, 2.2, 3.3, 4.0, 5.5};

    // Call the assembly procedure and store the result
    int mismatches = count_mismatches(array1, array2);

    // Print the result
    printf("Number of mismatches: %d\n", mismatches);

    return 0;
}
```
The application produces the following output:

Number of mismatches: 3

Example 11

In this example, we will calculate the mean, often referred to as the average, is a measure of central tendency that summarizes a set of data by identifying the central point within that dataset. It is calculated by adding up all the values in the dataset and then dividing by the number of values.

Formula for the Mean `$\mu$` for a dataset with values $(x_1, x_2, \ldots, x_n)$ is calculated as:

$$\mu = (x_1 + x_2 + \ldots + x_n) / n$$

For example, suppose we have the following dataset: (2, 4, 6, 8, 10).

Calculating the mean gives us

$$\mu = (2 + 4 + 6 + 8 + 10) / 5 = 30 / 5 = 6$$

Applications

The mean is widely used in various fields such as statistics, economics, finance, and general data analysis to provide a simple summary of the data. It helps to understand the overall level of the data and is often used in conjunction with other measures like the **median** and **mode** to get a comprehensive view of the dataset's characteristics.

Below is the RV32 assembly procedure (**Listing 21**) that calculates the Mean for a 5-element single-precision floating-point array.

Listing 21.

```
.section .text
.global calculate_mean
calculate_mean:
    addi sp, sp, -16        # Allocate stack space
    sw ra, 12(sp)           # Save return address
    sw a0, 8(sp)            # Save the pointer to the array
    li t0, 5                # Loop counter (5 elements)
    lw t1, 8(sp)            # Load base address of the array
    fmv.s.x fa1, zero        # Initialize sum to 0.0 (float)
  loop:
    beqz t0, end            # If counter is zero, exit loop
    flw fa0, 0(t1)          # Load current float element into fa0
    fadd.s fa1, fa1, fa0    # Add fa0 to the sum (fa1)
    addi t1, t1, 4          # Move to the next float element (4 bytes per float)
    addi t0, t0, -1         # Decrement loop counter
    j loop                  # Repeat the loop
  end:
    li t0, 5                # Load the number of elements (5) into t0
    fcvt.s.w fa0, t0        # Convert integer 5 to float and store in fa0
    fdiv.s fa1, fa1, fa0    # Divide the sum (fa1) by 5 to get the mean
    fmv.x.w a0, fa1         # Move the result (mean) from fa1 to a0

    lw ra, 12(sp)           # Restore return address
```

```
addi sp, sp, 16      # Restore stack pointer
ret                  # Return to caller
```

Explanation

Prologue: Adjust Stack Pointer:

```
addi sp, sp, -16
sw ra, 12(sp)
sw a0, 8(sp)
```

Allocate stack space and save the return address and the pointer to the array on the stack.

Set Up the Loop Counter and Base Address:

```
li t0, 5
lw t1, 8(sp)
fmv.s.x fa1, zero
```

Set the loop counter (**t0**) to 5 (since we have 5 elements), load the base address of the array into **t1**, and initialize the sum (**fa1**) to 0.0.

Loop to Sum the Elements:

```
loop:
  beqz t0, end
  flw fa0, 0(t1)
  fadd.s fa1, fa1, fa0
  addi t1, t1, 4
  addi t0, t0, -1
  j loop
```

In the loop, check if the loop counter is zero (`beqz t0, end`). If not, load the current float element into **fa0**, add **fa0** to the sum (**fa1**), move to the next element, and update the loop counter.

Calculate the Mean:

```
end:
```

```
li t0, 5
fcv.s.w fa0, t0
fdiv.s fa1, fa1, fa0
```

After summing the elements, load the number of elements (5) into **t0**, convert **t0** to a float (**fa0**), and divide the sum (**fa1**) by 5 to get the mean.

Return the Result:

```
fmv.x.w a0, fa1
lw ra, 12(sp)
addi sp, sp, 16
ret
```

Move the result (mean) from **fa1** to **a0**, restore the return address and stack pointer, and return to the caller.

The C code that calls the assembly procedure is shown below (**Listing 22**).

Listing 22.

```c
#include <stdio.h>

// Declaration of the assembly procedure
extern float calculate_mean(float* array);

int main() {
    // Initialize an array of 5 floating-point numbers
    float numbers[5] = {1.2, 2.3, 3.4, 4.5, 5.6};

    // Call the assembly procedure and store the result
    float mean = calculate_mean(numbers);

    // Print the result
    printf("Mean of the array: %f\n", mean);

    return 0;
}
```

The application produces the following output:

Mean of the array: 3.400000

Example 12

In this example, we consider how to calculate RMS using RV32 Assembly. RMS stands for Root Mean Square, and it is a statistical measure used to determine the magnitude of a varying quantity. It is especially useful in contexts where both positive and negative values occur, as it provides a measure of the average magnitude irrespective of the sign.

Calculation of RMS

The RMS value of a set of values x_1, x_2, ..., x_n is calculated using the following steps:
1. Square each value.
2. **Find the mean (average) of these squared values.**
3. **Take the square root of this mean.**

Mathematically, the RMS is given by:

$$RMS = \sqrt{[(x_1^2 + x_2^2 + \cdots + x_n^2)/n]}$$

Example

Consider the dataset: 2, 3, 1, 5, 4.
1. **Square each value:**

$$2^2 = 4,\ 3^2 = 9,\ 1^2 = 1,\ 5^2 = 25,\ 4^2 = 16$$

2. **Find the mean of these squared values:**

$$\text{Mean} = (4+9+1+25+16)/5 = 11$$

3. **Take the square root of this mean:**

$$RMS = \sqrt{11} \approx 3.32$$

Applications of RMS

4. **Electrical Engineering**: RMS values are used to calculate the effective value of alternating currents and voltages. For example, the RMS value of an AC voltage is the DC equivalent that would produce the same amount of heat in a resistor.
5. **Signal Processing**: RMS is used to quantify the magnitude of a varying signal. This is particularly useful for audio signals to measure their power.
6. **Statistics**: RMS is used as a measure of the magnitude of a set of values, irrespective of their sign. This is useful in various statistical analyses to describe the overall level of a dataset.
7. **Physics and Engineering**: RMS values are used to describe the average power of mechanical vibrations and waveforms.

Key Points

- RMS provides a single value that represents the magnitude of a set of values.
- It is particularly useful for datasets with both positive and negative values.
- It is widely used in fields where varying quantities are analyzed, such as engineering, physics, and statistics.

The RMS value is a robust measure for analyzing the magnitude of a varying quantity, providing meaningful insights in various practical and theoretical applications.

Let's go to the assembly procedure code **(Listing 23)** that calculates RMS using a 5-element single-precision floating-point array as a dataset.

Listing 23.

```
.section .text
.global calculate_rms
calculate_rms:
    addi sp, sp, -16      # Allocate stack space
    sw ra, 12(sp)         # Save return address
    sw a0, 8(sp)          # Save the pointer to the array
    li t0, 5              # Loop counter (5 elements)
    lw t1, 8(sp)          # Load base address of the array
    fmv.s.x fa1, zero     # Initialize sum of squares to 0.0 (float)
loop:
    beqz t0, end          # If counter is zero, exit loop
```

```
    flw fa0, 0(t1)          # Load current float element into fa0
    fmul.s fa2, fa0, fa0    # Square the element (fa0 * fa0)
    fadd.s fa1, fa1, fa2    # Add the square to the sum of squares (fa1)
    addi t1, t1, 4          # Move to the next float element (4 bytes per float)
    addi t0, t0, -1         # Decrement loop counter
    j loop                  # Repeat the loop
end:
    li t0, 5                # Load the number of elements (5) into t0
    fcvt.s.w fa0, t0        # Convert integer 5 to float and store in fa0
    fdiv.s fa1, fa1, fa0    # Divide the sum of squares (fa1) by 5 to get the
                            # mean of squares
    fsqrt.s fa1, fa1        # Take the square root of the mean of squares to get
                            # the RMS
    fmv.x.w a0, fa1         # Move the result (RMS) from fa1 to a0
    lw ra, 12(sp)           # Restore return address
    addi sp, sp, 16         # Restore stack pointer
    ret                     # Return to caller
```

Explanation

Prologue: Adjust Stack Pointer:

```
addi sp, sp, -16
sw ra, 12(sp)
sw a0, 8(sp)
```

Allocate stack space and save the return address and the pointer to the array on the stack.

Set Up the Loop Counter and Base Address:

```
li t0, 5
lw t1, 8(sp)
fmv.s.x fa1, zero
```

Set the loop counter (**t0**) to 5 (since we have 5 elements), load the base address of the array into **t1**, and initialize the sum of squares (**fa1**) to 0.0.

Loop to Sum the Squares of the Elements:

```
loop:
    beqz t0, end
    flw fa0, 0(t1)
    fmul.s fa2, fa0, fa0
    fadd.s fa1, fa1, fa2
    addi t1, t1, 4
    addi t0, t0, -1
    j loop
```

In the loop, check if the loop counter is zero (`beqz t0, end`). If not, load the current float element into **fa0**, square the element (**fa0 * fa0**), add the square to the sum of squares (**fa1**), move to the next element, and update the loop counter.

Calculate the Mean of Squares and the RMS

```
end:
    li t0, 5
    fcvt.s.w fa0, t0
    fdiv.s fa1, fa1, fa0
    fsqrt.s fa1, fa1
```

After summing the squares, load the number of elements (5) into **t0**, convert **t0** to a float (**fa0**), divide the sum of squares (**fa1**) by 5 to get the mean of squares, and then take the square root of the mean of squares to get the RMS.

Return the Result:

```
    fmv.x.w a0, fa1
    lw ra, 12(sp)
    addi sp, sp, 16
    ret
```

Move the result (RMS) from fa1 to a0, restore the return address and stack pointer, and return to the caller.

Here's the C code (**Listing 24**) to call the assembly procedure:

Listing 24.

```c
#include <stdio.h>

// Declaration of the assembly procedure
extern float calculate_rms(float* array);

int main() {
    // Initialize an array of 5 floating-point numbers
    float numbers[5] = {1.1, 2.2, 3.3, 4.4, 5.5};

    // Call the assembly procedure and store the result
    float rms = calculate_rms(numbers);

    // Print the result
    printf("RMS of the array: %f\n", rms);

    return 0;
}
```

The application produces the following output:

RMS of the array: 3.648287

Index

www.ingramcontent.com/pod-product-compliance
Lightning Source LLC
LaVergne TN
LVHW051703050326
832903LV00032B/3981